After Dinner Conversation Themes
Business Ethics Edition
Philosophy | Ethics Short Story Fiction

After Dinner Conversation *Themes* – Business Ethics

This magazine publishes fictional stories that explore ethical and philosophical questions in an informal manner. The purpose of these stories is to generate thoughtful discussion in an open and easily accessible manner.

Names, characters, businesses, organizations, places, events, and incidents are either the product of the author's imagination or are used fictitiously. Any resemblance to actual persons, living or dead, events, or locales is entirely coincidental. The magazine is published monthly in print and electronic format.

ISBN 979-8-9896194-8-1 (Print)
ISBN 979-8-2243563-9-3 (Digital)
Library of Congress Control Number: 2023952700

https://www.afterdinnerconversation.com

After Dinner Conversation believes humanity is improved by ethics and morals grounded in philosophical truth and that philosophical truth is discovered through intentional reflection and respectful debate. In order to facilitate that process, we have created a growing series of short stories across genres, a monthly magazine, and two podcasts. These accessible examples of abstract ethical and philosophical ideas are intended to draw out deeper discussions with friends, family, and students.

Table Of Contents

* * *

From the Edition Editor

There's no such thing as business ethics; there's just ethics.
Michael Josephson, American lawyer

For many, "business ethics" is an oxymoron. Two words that do not belong together. As the ten stories in this collection clearly demonstrate, there is an inherent–and sometimes blatant–conflict between the profit motive and the moral high ground. Doing the right thing can be a grey area.

Many of these stories grapple within that grey area. In "Claim," for example, an insurance agent is asked by a client to prepare a policy that will financially protect a church against claims of sexual abuse of children. It is a request that takes the protagonist back to her youth and up against a company logic that defends the right to honor the request.

Most of these stories go beyond the question of ethics to the impact of the decisions people make striving to be a good person and to be successful, often contradictory goals. "Bugs in the Valley" highlights the personal cost of doing the unethical, despite the business case that defends immoral actions.

What all these stories make crystal clear is that business and ethics are often at odds. There are no easy answers. Or are there?

donalee Moulton – Edition Editor

The Pool

Celia Lisset Alvarez

* * *

It had been about ten years since I'd driven down West Flagler. Even when Jack and I moved to Orlando, the apartment complexes on both sides of the street were already in disrepair. I still remember them when my parents and I moved here in 1974. They stretched from about 47th Avenue to 67th, all built more or less in the 1950s. Some were never works of art, but I always liked the circular one right on 47th or the one with the impressive two-story colonnade around 60-something. They were all usually one-bedroom apartments, no doubt built with the steno pool in mind. Speaking of pools, they all originally had one in the center court. By the late '70s, most of these had been filled in, paved over, turned into a grassy area, or—worst-case scenario—parking. There were rumors of a kid who'd been electrocuted during a thunderstorm. But the truth was less and more dramatic: with the wave of immigrants in the '60s, the buildings had become slums, and pools were expensive to keep up. And for what? The people who lived there had no time to sit in the sun.

Such a shame. There used to be a time when you could be poor and still entitled to a decent life. If I looked closely, I could still see the outlines of the pools. Cement borders around the ones that were a mess of yellow grass and weeds or cracks in the ones that had been paved over. Parked on. Forgotten.

I convinced Jack to buy me the one with the colonnade. At this point, we didn't need to profit from it. It could be my little project; I'd restore it to its original glory, pool and all, without raising the rents a cent. I didn't want anyone moving out or even moving in. I just wanted them, or maybe their kids, to have a place to take a swim or at least sit in the sun before or after going to work or school.

There was no such thing as a meeting. Some of the residents owned their apartments by this time, but I made it explicit in the letter I sent (in both English and Spanish) that the remodeling plans would not cost them anything. I did not expect the flood of requests I received: every apartment needed something, from new screens on the windows to new pipes, new appliances, more parking, an elevator that wouldn't trap someone at least once a month, bigger laundry and storage rooms. There were crumbling stairs and cracked tiles. Mold. Nobody mentioned a pool.

I made a list. I hired a contractor, a good one. We would start from the inside out: getting rid of mold (there was asbestos, too), leaks, termites. I put the residents up in hotels. Jack looked at the bills and raised his eyebrows, but that was all he did. It was the residents I had to fight—they did not want to get rid of their popcorn glitter ceilings or linoleum floors. Though they had wanted new appliances, they had not realized their new refrigerators would not be avocado green. They did not want their carpets pulled up. "You want to make all the apartments look the same," one of the older women, a widow who had lived there since the '70s, said. "I love my apartment just like it is." If not for the mold and termites, which put city codes on my side, I might not have been able to get anything done.

I discovered several first-floor dwellers had been feeding stray cats in the alleyway behind the building where the parking was. There were dozens of cats of all ages and breeds under cars, in the dumpster, skipping down the halls. I had them rounded up and fixed, vaccinated. Two more widows accosted me during one of my inspection visits, crying. "Animal!" They spat at me as if I had put them all down. There was a no-pets policy, but I have always loved and had pets, so I modified it. You could have up to two small pets per apartment, but you had to keep them inside. All you had to do was claim them from the shelter. Nobody did. I kept two of them for myself, a pair of calicos I named Hope and Faith.

I got rid of the rickety old elevator and installed two new ones on either side of the building. "I have to walk so much now to get to the elevator," one of the tenants who lived in the middle of the building complained. She was in her eighties and used a walker.

"But you live on the first floor," I said. "Why do you need to use the elevator?"

"My daughter lives on the second floor."

There was nothing I could do about that. But I added a new laundry room on the second floor and a second storage room on the first in vacant apartments. Although they cost a fortune, Jack was okay with the impact windows and doors because we got a big discount on the insurance.

Finally, we began on the pool.

"When is all this noise going to stop?" one of the men complained. "We have been living in terror for months."

The pool was originally quite large, oval, with a surrounding stone courtyard where there could be tables and loungers. It would have to be smaller this time, the contractor explained. We would never pass inspection unless we installed a safety railing around it.

"A safety railing?" I asked. I pictured what it would look like. Hideous. When I was a kid, my godparents lived in one of these buildings. We didn't have safety railings around pools. Your father would pick you up and throw you in the deep end. That's how you learned how to swim. Sure, some kids drowned when no one was watching. But usually, there was always someone watching. Now there was no getting around it. Parents couldn't be trusted. No railing, no pool. I caved. It was still pretty big.

The courtyard around it should not be stone, Mitch, the contractor, argued. "Too unstable," he said. "Too many elderly residents. It's a lawsuit waiting to happen."

"Okay," I said. I trusted Mitch and had become used to compromising at this point. "What do you suggest? Nothing too expensive." Jack's eyebrows were reaching his hairline by now, and that had receded significantly.

"Well," Mitch said, scratching his head. "I guess that puts tile out of the question. Concrete. We can dye it, stamp it, whatever you want. I got a guy." Luckily Mitch had lots of guys. Once, I had gone with him to Home Depot early on a Saturday. He held up three fingers out his window, and three guys leaped into the back of his pickup. They didn't even ask what kind of work they'd be doing or how much they'd get paid.

Soon, the pool was finished.

Jack had to travel to Washington right around that time, and I'd gone with him, so I'd missed the grand reveal. I wasn't able to make it down to Miami until the pool had been in use for a few weeks.

Driving up to the building, I looked expectantly out the window, craning my neck for the first glimpse of the pool. I had purposely gone around noon on a Saturday, thinking that would be the most likely day for the residents to be enjoying it. To my surprise, the pool was deserted. It had definitely been used, however. Towels flapped in the wind from the balconies on both sides. Leaves floated on the water. Empty soda cans, beer bottles, and fast-food packages littered the tables I had arranged around the pool, and one of the loungers was on its side.

I sent a letter. In English and Spanish.

In response to complaints about the cost of putting the towels in the dryers, I had the coin slots removed. But more complaints kept coming. Someone on the second floor had adopted two little yapping terriers that barked all day while she was at work. Dog shit had been found on the grass border around the pool courtyard. The men were smoking in the pool area, and the mothers were concerned about their children inhaling all that secondhand smoke. Signs had to be put up.

I got a call around midnight one Sunday. I was in Orlando. It was from Dolores, the lady in her eighties from the first-floor center apartment. Her living room window had a clear view of the pool.

"I can't sleep!" she screamed. "Those kids are still out

there. They're smoking pot! I can smell it from here, and it's making me sick!"

I called Ernesto, the super. "Okay," he said, "but this is not my job. You should call the police."

"I don't want to call the police," I said. "These are my tenants. Besides, Dolores says they're just kids."

"Just kids? Tenants, eh?" Ernesto said sarcastically. "Look, Ms. Carrie, one or two of these 'kids' might be your tenants, but what you got out there is a gang."

"What?"

"You heard me. Tattoos. Piercings. Loud music. Drugs. I wouldn't be surprised if they were armed."

"Jesus," I said. "Just please try asking them to leave nicely. If they don't comply, you can call the police."

Ernesto called the police. Turns out none of them were my tenants. They had just snuck in. Some of them were minors. The police suggested we put a locked gate around the property. Jack's eyebrows retreated into his hair.

But that was not the worst of it.

Before Ernesto went to confront the thugs (that was Jack's word), if he ever did (I suspect he called the police from the safety of his apartment), Dolores took it upon herself to get rid of the pests on her own. She put on her housecoat and ambled to the pool area, pushing her walker in her slippers.

She slid on a puddle and fell on the concrete.

I first heard of it around 1:00 a.m. from her daughter, Patricia, who called me from the hospital. My first thought was a broken hip, instant death, but it was a broken shoulder. "I hope you're happy," Patricia said. "Eighty-two and had never broken a bone in her life." She held the phone so I could hear Dolores screaming. It was loud.

Of course, there was a lawsuit. Luckily, we were able to settle out of court, but Jack had had it. "What exactly are you getting out of this, Carrie?" he finally said. Dolores had to go to a rehab facility. I was crying. "It seems like nothing but aggravation."

I hired an assistant for Ernesto. He came in every day at sunset to clean up around the pool and lock the gate. Nothing else happened for about another three months, other than the usual complaints about there not being enough parking. To make room for the pool again, I had been forced to restrict the parking to one spot per apartment and only two visitor spots. In the interim, Dolores had returned. "My grandchildren have no place to park, so they don't come to visit me anymore."

Also, Ernesto noticed that tenants from the nearby apartment buildings were using our laundry rooms. I reinstalled the coin slots. The towels returned to the balconies.

It was around 8:00 p.m. in mid-July when I got the call from Lalo, the kid I'd hired to keep the pool area safe. I was spending the summer in Miami with family, so when he said, "I think you need to come over," I did.

There was a burlap bag at the bottom of the pool.

"What is it?" I asked Lalo.

He was a skinny kid, very brown, always in board shorts, no shoes. He gave me a look. I noticed his hair was wet. "I didn't know if I should bring it up or what," he said.

"Please," I asked.

He dove into the pool without hesitation. Whatever was in the bag was heavy; he struggled to bring it up. When he got to the edge of the pool, he swung the bag onto the concrete. It landed with a dull thud. Then he scrambled out and knelt in front of it. It was tied with a white rope. "You sure you want to see this?" he asked.

"You called me over, didn't you?" I was getting a little exasperated. I could feel my heart pumping in my chest. I couldn't guess what was in the bag, but it couldn't be anything good.

Lalo nodded, untied the rope, and held the bag open for me to look. I bent over and gasped. It was the two yapping terriers and a bunch of rocks. Not rocks. Concrete. Pieces of the concrete that had once filled the pool, which the contractors had failed to completely haul away and had been littering the parking lot for months.

"Take them away," I said.

"What do you want—"

"Just take them away—I don't care—figure it out."

* * *

I suppose it was Lalo or Ernesto who found the dogs' owner and delivered the news. There was an animal cruelty report filed, but, of course, no one was ever charged.

I remember when we moved out of our first apartment in this country. It was right after the front lawn got paved. We moved to a duplex just a few blocks away. It was still just a 1/1. We were still renting. At the time, I couldn't understand the decision.

"Just sell it," I told Jack, who was more than happy to do so. I didn't return to Miami for a long time until my godmother died, the one who had lived in the apartment building with the pool when I was little. She, too, had eventually moved to a duplex and then bought a house in Westchester. After my godfather died, she moved into a condo complex—with a pool. By that time, she was too old to use it. It was hard for her to walk, and it was always so hot.

* * *

This story first appeared in the After Dinner Conversation—September 2023 issue.

Discussion Questions

1. Was Carrie (*the property owner*) wrong to want to fix up the complex and make it nicer? Should she have simply left the complex in its dilapidated state and focused on making money from it? Should she have evicted everyone, renovated the empty complex, and gotten all new tenants?

2. When the units were being remodeled, the tenants complained the new refrigerator wasn't 1970s avocado green and that the shag carpet was replaced with new flooring concepts. Why weren't the residents more grateful for the housing upgrades?

3. How do you know when complaints from your tenants are worth listening to and when they should be ignored? Which tenant complaints in the story were legitimate, and which should have been ignored?

4. At what point, *if any*, in the complex renovation process should Carrie have met with the tenants to hear their thoughts and feedback? Why didn't she?

5. Inertia and resistance to change—even seemingly positive change—dominate tenants' attitudes. What lessons, if any, from Carrie's renovations could be applied to city, state, and national governments trying to make positive policy changes?

* * *

First Gold

Bob Beach

* * *

"Hey, Evan, you missed all the excitement Saturday night." Connor McKee stood at the opening to Evan Moore's cubicle, making faces at the mug of bitter agency coffee in his hand. "I can't believe you didn't show!"

Evan didn't look up from his monitor. "The in-laws are in town. Dana's dad insisted on taking us out to Mancy's and the symphony." Not only did he miss the Ad Club dinner, he had to spend the night listening to the old bastard wail about the lamestream media and their fake news.

"You skipped the awards dinner for your in-laws? Wow, that's dedication. Anyway, congratulations, man, that's terrific! Nice piece!" He turned to leave.

"Congratulations? What for?" Evan lifted his head from Adobe Illustrator, where he was putting the finishing touches on a logo design for Hanover Construction.

"The award. Didn't you know? You got a gold medal Saturday!"

Evan's heart locked up and his mouth went dry. A gold? Me? He spun around on his chair. But then he remembered he hadn't entered anything.

"I did? What for?"

"Yeah, a gold medal. For the Atkins poster."

Evan felt an icy hand grab his spine. Not the Atkins poster. No. He had that handled. "But I didn't enter that. I had Kathy pull it."

"Well, lucky for you she didn't pull hard enough—it got a gold. Your first, isn't it?"

"Jesus Christ." Evan jumped up and waddled across the bullpen toward Kathy's office. The large, open area was dimly lighted to avoid screen glare and distraction for the designers. Although he never found it a distraction and wondered if the real reason wasn't just to save on electricity. For privacy, the space was divided into small cubicles with five-foot fabric-covered walls, which gave about as much privacy as a half-open bathroom door.

A half dozen designers tapped intently away at their keyboards. Oversize screens flashed and beeped and belched video into the semi-darkness as he passed. A colony of moles sifting for precious metals: gold, silver, bronze.

"Hey, Evan, congratulations!" called someone from a cubicle.

He popped his head into Kathy's doorway. The administrative staff had their own individual offices, with four walls and a door that actually closed, as though they were more important to the agency than the designers who created the product. "Didn't you pull the Atkins poster from the entry pile?"

Kathy looked up and nodded. "Yeah. Isn't that what you

wanted?"

"How could it win an award, then?"

"Damn, it did, didn't it?" Kathy thought a moment. "The client must have entered it himself. It was somebody from Atkins that accepted the award. Congratulations, by the way. Is that your first gold?"

By the time she was finished speaking, Evan was halfway back to his workstation. Crap. The first gold was the passage to manhood as a designer, the coming of age, the signaling of a future star. Something he chased as hard as any of the other creatives. But this sure as hell wasn't the way to do it. If only he hadn't been so wiped out. If only he'd had more time. This would hang over his head for a month, maybe longer, until he was sure nobody had caught on. Well, hell—everybody did it. Why should he sweat?

Connor had moved on by the time he got back to his cubicle. Evan watched him drift through the bullpen, looking more like an account executive than a writer, with his tailored jackets and Stephano Ricci ties. Connor was tall and slim, built for fashion. Evan Moore was less tall (he didn't like the word *short*) and burly (he didn't like the word *pudgy*) and his closet was filled with X sizes in heavy fabric, like denim shirts and pants, to disguise unflattering bulges. On the positive side, denim wore like iron and only needed washing once a month or so. And denim was never out of style in the bullpen.

The Atkins poster was going to be a problem. Evan wasn't among the creative stars of the agency and everybody knew it. He was a competent designer but not brilliant, certainly not anyone's candidate to win a gold medal at the ad show. In fact, this might be his only chance to snag a medal of any kind, ever.

He never dreamed that piece would win an award, but damn! If nobody caught on, it would be so cool to have just one really great design in his portfolio, one big award. Even if it wasn't really his.

Evan settled down again to the Hanover logo. When this was finished, he'd have a set of four alternative designs to hand to the account guy—Webster had been nagging him about this for three days. His mouse flew around the pad, adding line, color, typography. In a moment, the problem of the Atkins poster faded away and the soft background murmur of the bullpen faded.

This version of the Hanover design was a three-dimensional block "H" in perspective that looked formed of concrete. He'd found a terrific color combination—a medium grayish-green face with the sides and top in a slightly darker grayish blue—very contemporary, a sophisticated look. But it wouldn't work. There wasn't enough contrast between the colors to reproduce well in black and white, like in the newspaper. The form of the "H" would disappear. And it was too soft—a construction company should have a bolder, stronger image. He changed the blue to a heavy green, almost black, working as a dark shadow to emphasize the lighter green face. Better. The "H" really popped, now. He usually considered green a weak color, but Hanover was a residential builder and the green suggested natural forms, landscaping, nature. Positive associations for a prospective residential client. He fiddled with the lighter green, making it brighter and trying subtly different hues. Gradually, the design came alive, and the 34" x 22" CRT screen of his monitor became Evan's entire universe.

"Congratulations, Evan. Your first gold. You've raised the

bar for yourself!" Paul Wick, the creative director, draped his lanky body over Evan's cubicle wall, and suddenly the Atkins problem was in his face again.

Crap. Was that going to be another issue? Were expectations going to be higher after this? He glanced at his watch. Noon already. Almost three hours had passed while Evan was lost in the ecstasy of creation.

"Hey, Paul."

"All the medal winners are going out to lunch to celebrate," said Paul. "On me. Grumpy's. Grab your hat."

That was all Evan needed—stuck at a table for an hour, with the agency's top creatives grilling him about his award. "Ah, shit, Paul, I can't. I've got this logo to finish up and get mounted for a presentation at one."

Paul looked surprised, then offended. "Seriously? Can't spare an hour?"

"I'd better not, Paul. Webster's been on my ass about this. Sorry."

"Lord love a duck. Since when has work replaced fun as Priority One around here? Okay, but you know what happens when you don't show—we're all going to make fun of your little pecker." He stood up and walked away.

Yeah, the Atkins poster was going to be a problem. But what could he do about it? He could confess now, but that would seal his fate. And kill his one chance—a ridiculous, impossible chance—for a gold medal. Let it ride. And hope.

* * *

Evan wheeled his Ford Escort to the curb in front of his house. Daddy had parked his mammoth GMC Yukon in the driveway, so Evan couldn't get to the garage. Why did he need all that horsepower and those big, knobby tires to haul two wrinkled boomers and a sack of groceries back and forth from Kroger? The closest Daddy ever got to off-road driving was the unpaved parking lot at the church of the holy rollers. And not even then if it was raining.

Evan climbed the front steps to the porch. The house was a three-bedroom wood frame in the university area of west Toledo. Back in the day, the neighborhood was primarily Jewish and the homes were all neatly painted, the lawns groomed. But the makeup of the area had changed. Now worn patches of bare dirt appeared here and there, and most of the homes needed touching up. Clusters of kids played stickball and soccer in the street. But that was the reason Evan could afford it now. He pushed open the front door.

"Surprise!"

It was. Evan stopped, feet frozen in place. Dana stood just inside the door wearing a long-striped cooking apron over her good red dress, holding a bright yellow cake sprinkled with gold flakes. Her parents flanked her, holding bunches of helium-filled balloons by their strings. Dana and her mother were beaming and Daddy's perpetual frown had softened a bit. What the hell? This wasn't his birthday. The cake had a small centerpiece—a tennis trophy? No, just a plastic ceremonial cup with big handles. A gold cup. He looked up at the balloons. Gold. They'd found out somehow. Crap. The more people that knew about this, the more likely things could get out of hand.

Dana's mother, Lydia, rushed forward and threw her arms around his neck in a big hug.

"Oh, Evan, we're all so proud of you."

Lydia was plump and gray but hid it well with bright,

frilly outfits. Daddy was wiry and erect as a goalpost, with silver hair in a short brushback and a pencil-thin mustache like the British officers in old war movies. He hated denim almost as much as he hated hair that came down past the shirt collar, as he reminded Evan daily. He probably hated Evan, too, but hadn't specifically articulated that yet.

Daddy stuck his hand out tentatively. "Congratulations, Evan." He didn't seem quite ready to accept that Evan had achieved something notable. Probably a clerical mistake somewhere that would be corrected in due time.

Evan took his hand and gave it a squeeze. "Thanks, Don."

Dana, not wanting to mash the cake, just stood there grinning and brushing stylishly long strands of dark hair from her face.

Evan felt his face growing warm and hoped it wasn't turning red. What was the problem? Why the guilt or shame or embarrassment, whatever the hell it was? He did it all the time. Everybody did. But he hadn't been careful this time. And it won a medal.

When Lydia and Daddy had disengaged, Dana grabbed his arm with one hand and propelled him into the dining room. "Keri Wick called this morning to see why we weren't there Saturday night. She told me about your gold medal. Congratulations, star designer!" She pulled out the chair at the head of the table and set the cake down.

The aroma of grilling steak drifted in the door as Dana made her way out to the patio. Definitely a celebration. Although the steak was really for Daddy. Evan and Dana didn't spring for steak very often, but Daddy didn't consider it a meal unless there was meat.

The good plates and glasses, the ones that matched, were set. That was real butter on the table. Uh-oh. There was a bottle of wine, a dark red, probably a cabernet. For the celebration, obviously—Evan and Dana didn't usually have wine with meals and Evan was mostly a beer drinker. But Daddy with a bottle of anything was risky business.

Already on the table were plates of asparagus, tomato and mozzarella salad, red potatoes, and dinner rolls. The aroma of the freshly baked cake still lingered in the air.

Lydia slid into a chair at the table. "Oh, this all looks just so delicious!"

"Just what is it you do again, Evan?" asked Daddy. Evan explained at least once each time they visited, but Daddy had never seemed to grasp it.

"I'm a graphic designer, Don."

"So show me something you've designed."

Evan pulled out a magazine from the stack on the side table and flipped through to an ad for Ithaca shotguns, something he thought the old bastard might appreciate. "Here. This is one of my ads."

Daddy took the magazine and nodded and hemmed to himself for a minute. "So you did the picture of the shotgun?"

"No. that was the photographer."

"How about this picture of the bird in the air? That's pretty."

"No, the illustrator did that."

"Did you write the words?" asked Daddy.

"No. The copywriter wrote the words."

"How about this little thing? The logo, is it?"

"No, they've had that for years. It's an icon of the

industry."

"An icon, an icon..." he muttered to himself, hemming some more. He put the magazine down. The unasked question hung in the air: So if you didn't do any of those, and there's nothing else on the page, what the fuck exactly did you do?

"Look, Don, I'm the one who determines what the ad is all about. Maybe it doesn't sound like much, but nothing happens—not the pictures, not the words—until I've decided what goes into the ad, what it will look like and where things go on the page."

Daddy picked up the magazine and perused the ad again. "So you're the one who decides that the pictures should go at the top and the words go at the bottom."

Evan felt his face starting to burn. He was sure Daddy was pimping him—nobody could really be that dense. But the old goat was clever. Evan couldn't come right and accuse him or Dana and her mom would be all over his case.

Dana chuffed through the kitchen door in a cloud of smoke and sizzle, balancing a plate of juicy steaks in her kitchen mitts.

"Whoa!" said Daddy, in his best imitation of Robert Mitchum. "Beef—it's what's for dinner!"

Everybody sat for Daddy's prayer. Then there was a shuffle as serving platters made their way around the table and the steaks and side dishes were doled out, sorted, sampled and praised. Daddy uncorked the wine and poured for everyone.

"A toast," he said, holding up his glass. "To the star designer. First gold but not the last!"

"Hear, hear," said Lydia.

"To my talented husband!" said Dana.

Lydia and Dana raised their glasses and touched Daddy's. Evan followed reluctantly.

Daddy drained half his glass and topped it off again.

They dug into their dinner, and for a few moments there was only the sound of cutting, chewing and the occasional murmur of appreciation.

"The steak is absolutely perfect, honey," said Lydia. "Don't you think so, dear?"

Daddy grunted. "Could have pulled it off the fire a little sooner. Still, nothing like steak for a real dinner."

"Speaking of real," said Dana. "I suppose this is a ridiculous question, Mom, but have you tried the new Impossible Burgers? They're actually good. You can hardly tell the difference."

"You mean fake meat?" said Daddy. "You're right, it is a ridiculous question. Just some left-wing idea to put the cattle ranchers out of business." Daddy finished his glass of wine and poured another.

"Are they really that good?" asked Lydia.

"This one is," said Evan. "It's really getting popular. Even Don couldn't tell the difference."

Don frowned.

"Throw on a little mustard, pickle, onion... they even bleed like real meat, like a regular fast-food burger. You can get it at BK."

"What's this liberal rush to dictate how we live our lives?" said Daddy. "I don't want fake meat, I want real meat. And I want light bulbs like Edison made, toilets you don't have to flush four times and a car you don't have to plug in at a charging station every fifteen minutes."

"Daddy, nobody's dictating how you live your life," said Dana. "You eat real meat every day, you have incandescent bulbs in every room and you have the old kind of toilets that waste water. Just the way you want it. Nobody's even asking you to change."

"The damn president is! The cows are farting too much methane so he's going to ban red meat to fight global warming. Another goddamn hoax. Just more fake news to force their socialist agenda on us."

Evan rolled his eyes and wiped his mouth with his napkin to hide the smirk.

"Oh, Don," said Lydia.

Daddy was getting red in the face, and he refilled his wineglass.

"How about Rush and Beck and Newsmax, Don? Or Fox and their chattering heads? That's the real fake news," said Evan.

Daddy wadded up his napkin and threw it on the table. "It's their own opinions. They have a right to express that! It's their freedom of speech."

"They're spouting ridiculous, baseless claims that mislead people," said Evan. "Don't you think they have a responsibility to tell the truth?"

Dana stood up abruptly. "Anybody want coffee?" She walked around the table grabbing plates, empty or not. Time to douse the flames of political passion before it got out of hand. "Daddy, how about you?"

Daddy ignored her and emptied the last of the cabernet into his glass.

"Evan, would you give me a hand clearing the table?"

"I'll help you, honey," said Lydia, springing to her feet.

"This was a wonderful dinner."

For a moment there was only the clattering of dishes and plates and dinnerware as Evan and Dana and Lydia gathered the remains of the meal and headed for the kitchen.

Daddy glared at their departing backs and lifted his glass. "Well, there's your truth and then there's *my* truth."

Evan looked up at the ceiling in supplication and lifted his arms.

Dana leaned against him and put her arms around his waist.

"You sure he's your real father?" whispered Evan. "There wasn't a libbie in the woodpile somewhere?"

Dana punched him in the side. "I'm sorry your celebration didn't go well, sweetie."

"It was a great meal, though. Thank you." He gave her a squeeze. "Listen," he murmured. "About that. Go easy on this medal thing, okay? Don't tell your friends or neighbors about it. Just pretend it never happened."

Dana stiffened and stepped back. "Why? This is great news! I want everybody to know what a terrific designer my husband is. Why should I keep quiet?"

"Look, it's a mistake. I got the medal, but I don't deserve it. I don't want people to think I'm a grasping jerk if they should find out."

Dana's eyes widened. "What? Why? What did you do?"

Evan sneaked a glance toward the living room, where Daddy and Lydia were just beginning their nightly scrap. "Keep it down, okay? I copied the idea for the poster. It accidentally got entered."

"So what? You do that all the time. You spend hours

browsing through that stack of design magazines in the den looking for ideas."

"But this time I lifted the whole thing. No changes. I didn't have time. And I never wanted it entered in the show."

"Oh, don't be silly. If it wasn't for those books, you designers would never get any ideas. Nobody's going to care. Most of those books are years old, anyway—the original client won't give a damn. You worry too much."

Damn. He might as well take out an ad in the newspaper. The newspaper! Holy crap! *The Blade* would cover the story, they did every year. There was no way to keep a lid on it.

But Dana didn't think it was a big deal. Maybe nobody else would, either. Still, it was time to test the water on this, just in case.

* * *

When he got to his workstation the next morning, Harper Levin was sitting in his chair reading the coverage of the show in *The Blade*. Harper was the agency's top designer and a mentor of sorts to less stellar lights like Evan. She was petite with lots of dark hair and startling green eyes. Harper was one of the few designers in the bullpen who dressed up for work, usually pants suits with frilly blouses. Marking her territory as alpha creative, with an eye on Wick's job.

This was it. Either he laid it all out now to Harper or duck and roll. But if he didn't come clean now and everything unraveled later, he'd be toast. They'd think it was an intentional steal. Harper was his cover, evidence that it was all a mistake. And maybe, just maybe, it would end with her and he could quietly keep his gold.

"Too bad you weren't there Saturday," said Harper. "You

missed an opportunity to get your face in the paper. Can't pass those up. Looks good in your personnel file."

Well, at least he'd gotten a break there. "Hey, listen, Harper, about that poster—"

"You're one up on me so far this year. I got stiffed. Your first gold, right?"

"Yeah, about that. I need your advice."

"Good. I've got plenty of that, and it's all free. One: don't go looking to sign with a talent agency quite yet. Makes management nervous and you don't have the resume to attract BBD&O. Two: stay away from the groupies—they're nothing but trouble."

"Yeah, no worries there. Thanks." He pulled up the side chair next to Harper and pulled up a PDF image of the Atkins poster.

"That's your gold," she said, and clapped her hands in applause.

He reached into a drawer and pulled out a design magazine. *OZ Grafix*, a twenty-year-old Australian publication, something he'd found at the bottom of a pile in the resource library. He handed it to Harper. "Page twenty-three."

Harper flipped to the page. "Oh, shit."

Evan's design was an exact copy of the poster in the magazine.

"This one's by… Adrian Smith. In *Australia*?" She looked up at Evan. "Couldn't you at least have changed the colors? Jesus, Evan, what were you thinking?"

"Yeah, I know. But it was like two in the morning and the client needed it at nine. I'd been working on the project all day and I was out of gas. I had two solid designs but I needed another, so I tossed in a swipe. Only one chance in three he'd pick it."

"That was your first mistake," said Harper.

"What's that?"

"Clients have an uncanny nose for crap. You give the client a couple solid designs and a turkey to choose from and the client will pick the turkey every time! Or, in this case, the swipe."

She was right. A law of client behavior he'd forgotten in his exhaustion.

"But fuck, you shouldn't have entered it," she said. "It's unethical. Not to mention really stupid. This could make the whole agency look bad. Wick will blow a gasket!"

"I *didn't* enter it. I had Kathy pull it. But the client loved it so much he entered it himself! I didn't know about it until after the show."

Harper's eyes widened, then she burst out laughing. She covered her mouth. "I'm sorry. But that's just so... so... weird. So funny!"

Evan scowled. "Everybody does it."

"I know, I know. But we usually diddle with it a bit first." She started laughing again.

"So what should I do? Tell Wick? Or ignore it and hope nobody catches on?"

Her face turned sober again. "Shit, don't tell Wick. Nobody's gonna go Googling around in Australia, for Christ's sake. And this thing is twenty years old. Bury it." She tossed the magazine into the wastebasket. "Just keep your ass clean, okay? No more shortcuts. I don't want to have to train any more rookies." Harper got up and walked out.

Good. Harper thought it was a joke. If anybody else got wind of it, maybe they would, too. If they didn't, he'd be marked as the guy who claimed a medal for somebody else's piece. And Evan didn't want this first gold to be a rite of passage to a new line of work.

* * *

The next two weeks crawled by like his great-aunt Lucy on her Sunday drive to church. Each day Evan expected to find a summons to Wick's office, but each time he passed Paul in the bullpen he got nothing more than a friendly wave. He began to breathe again. He kept his head down and his mouth shut, trying to be invisible. As the days passed, it looked like he might actually get away with it. His own gold medal.

On Thursday of the third week, he received a letter from the Advertising Club of Toledo:

* * *

Dear Mr. Moore,

It has come to our attention that the poster design for the Atkins Company, which was submitted to the recent awards show listing you as designer, was directly copied from a poster designed by Adrian Smith of Brisbane, Queensland, Australia and published in the magazine *OZ Grafix*. We are therefore rescinding the gold medal award issued to you and demanding the return of the certificate.

Under no circumstances can we countenance such unethical and blatant plagiarism. It brings disgrace not only upon you, but upon the Advertising Club of Toledo. Please return the certificate immediately. In addition, we are permanently barring you from any and all Toledo Advertising Club events in the future.

Sincerely,

Andrea Watson, Executive Director

At the bottom of the letter was a hand-scribbled note:

Evan: We know ideas get swiped every day. If you hadn't won a gold medal, we could have let this slide. But given the complaint, we had to do this. Sorry. – Andrea

* * *

It was over. Gossip like this would spread faster than a poison ivy rash. By morning, the whole world would know. The cheater. The copycat. Everything he did from now on would be questioned, scrutinized. If he ever did manage to win anything, people would snicker in disbelief behind his back. In an industry where creative awards helped determine salaries, he was doomed to fall to the bottom of the ladder.

Who was the whistleblower? Who could possibly have known about a twenty-year-old Australian graphics magazine? Was it somebody from Metzger who'd seen this in the file? Harper, even? No, he was no threat to her. But who?

Better that Wick hear it from Evan now than from the grapevine tomorrow. He pulled himself out of his chair and trudged across the room to Paul's office. He rapped on the door.

"Hey, Evan. What's up?"

Evan stepped in and tossed the letter and the magazine on his desk. Although Paul had his own office, it was dimly lighted like the rest of the creative department. Even creative directors had workstations and quotas for billable hours. Paul picked the letter up and read it through, then read it again. He dropped the letter on the desk and leaned back in his chair. "Show me."

Evan sat at Paul's computer and brought up the image of

his poster. "Page twenty-three," he said.

Paul flipped to page twenty-three, leaned forward and stared. "Jesus Christ, Evan. You know better than this. If you're gonna steal a design, you have to change the colors or flip it or reverse it or change the font. Or something. Preferably all of the above. What the fuck?" He glared up at Evan.

"Paul, it's a twenty-year-old book from Australia, for God's sake. It was a rush job and it was late and I was exhausted. And I needed a third design. The rule is a minimum of three. I thought I'd have a chance to work it a bit when it came back, but he loved it just the way it was."

"But entering it? Claiming it as your own?"

"I know, I know. When I heard it was in the submission pile I pulled it. But then the client submitted it *himself*. He picked up the award. I wasn't even there that night."

The anger faded from Paul's face and he gave a long, low whistle. "Holy crap! That's a new one."

"I mean, everybody does this," said Evan. "I never thought there was a chance in hell it would float to the top. And that's what the whole reference library you've got in there is for, isn't it? All those journals and award show books. To spark ideas. Or swipe something—that's what it amounts to. Everybody calls it the swipe file."

"And what's the chance, right?" said Paul. "Everything's so arbitrary, so subjective, another set of judges and this probably wouldn't even have made the cut. Talk about bad breaks." He sat up in his chair and tossed the letter back toward Evan. "Just give them back their fucking certificate. Like you say, everybody does it." He pointed his finger at Evan. "Just don't pull any more shit like this. If Haydon finds out, I'll have to poke him down off the ceiling with a stick!"

"I don't have the certificate. The client picked it up at the show."

Wick threw himself back in his chair. "Oh, fuck."

"So, what do I do?"

Wick thought for a moment and sat up. "Don't worry about it. I'll have the account guy talk to the client. Schmooze him a little, get the certificate back. His piece won a fucking award, he should be happy as a mutt with a fresh bone."

Terrific. But it was Evan who'd have to live with the bad press and the lifetime ban. He'd probably have to stay at Metzger Advertising his whole fucking life. Who else would hire him now?

* * *

"Hey, bad break with the Atkins poster," said Connor. He hung over the divider with the ever-present mug of coffee. "Too bad about the gold. Man, what a crazy deal."

"Yeah," said Evan.

"This will all blow over by next year, trust me. The Ad Club people will forget or they won't give a damn. Probably both, as long as nobody's yanking their chain."

"Yeah."

"Well, don't worry about it. You'll survive." Connor meandered through the bullpen to impress some other unsuspecting designer with his threads.

"Yeah."

Maybe Connor was right—nobody cared enough to make a deal of it. But some people had long memories. And whoever turned him in would still be around. And how many people would just read the headline and ignore the explanation buried in the fine print?

The brutal fact was that his career options had narrowed considerably. So had his earning power. For the immediate future, he was the black sheep of the ad community. And trying something else? Leaving the business? Unthinkable. This was his life, his love. But he still had a good job. Maybe his colleagues would see it as a joke, like Harper, or an awkward accident like Connor. He wouldn't have to wait long to find out.

* * *

Evan waited a week.

"Haydon wants to see me? Haydon Metzger?"

The president wanted to see Evan? Only one thing this could be about. Evan hung up the phone and shuffled through the creative department across the building to the administrative offices on the far side. More like a bank or an attorney's office over here. Carpeting and secretaries and big walnut desks and thick glass doors to the offices and bright LED lights all over so you could see what you were doing. He stopped in front of the secretary's desk.

"Go on in, Evan," she said with a broad smile. "He's expecting you."

What big teeth you have, Grandma. He rapped on the glass door and stepped inside.

Metzger looked up and waved him in. "Come on in, Evan. Have a seat."

Evan sat without a word. There was a white envelope sitting on Metzger's desk. Metzger leaned back in his chair and scratched his head.

"I'm sure you know what this is about. And I have to tell you, I've never come across anything like this before. This thing has grown from a simple oversight to an irritation to a pain in the ass quicker than anything I've ever seen." He sat up in his chair again, put his elbows on the desk and steepled his fingers.

Just a pain in the ass? That didn't sound too bad.

"Anyway, we got your certificate back."

His certificate? Maybe Metzger didn't realize that he'd never laid eyes on it.

"We'll return it to the Ad Club, so don't worry about that. But Tom Atkins was extremely unhappy about it. He thought he was being cheated, that we were billing him for the creation of a design that was just lifted from somewhere else."

"But he actually got a deal," said Evan. "I didn't record the four or five hours it would have taken to design it from scratch. Just the half hour it took to scan and trace the original. He came out ahead."

Metzger nodded. "I know. We all understand. But his real problem was the publicity over a pirated design. He feels he's been made a fool of by this agency in front of the whole community. He's unhappy and unreasonable."

"But he's got a design he loves," said Evan. "It'll do a good job for him."

"In his current mood, that's irrelevant."

He was being fired. Evan was losing his job over something everybody in the industry did. Where would he go?

"I'm sorry as hell about this. It's our loss even more than it is yours."

Evan doubted that. Where would the money come from to cover the bills? How long would it take him to find another design job?

"But I'm sure you can understand, even if you don't agree.

We can't keep you after this. He's a good client. Not a huge one, but a very profitable one. He's threatened to pull his account. He wants blood, and we have to give it to him."

Evan's blood, of course. He could hear it pounding in his ears even now. Would any other agency even give him an interview? Did the scandal mean he was poison in the ad world, now?

"Technically, his position is solid—we submitted a stolen design and charged him for it. He has a legitimate beef. We have no ground to stand on, here. I'm sorry."

Metzger stood and picked up the envelope from the desk. He walked around to Evan. Evan stood up and Metzger put the envelope in his hands.

"There's four weeks of severance here, twice what we usually give. And an excellent letter of reference. We hate to lose you, Evan. You've been a good employee for us, and that's what we'll tell anyone who wants to contact us. But we can't afford to lose an account over this silly thing. Technically, this was unethical behavior—copying somebody else's design and presenting it as yours—so that's what it will read on the record. But we all know better—it was just a bad break."

Technically? Silly thing? Bad break? It was nice that this didn't cause Metzger to lose any sleep, but what was he was supposed to tell Dana?

"We'll clean out your workstation and send all your personal things home to you."

He put his hand on Evan's shoulder and turned him toward the door. "I wouldn't worry about finding another job if I were you. You'll catch on with somebody. A week, two weeks tops. You're too good to be on the street longer than that. You might even end up with a better position. You'll have a good reference. The other agencies will understand—it won't be a deal-breaker. After all, everybody does it."

* * *

This story first appeared in the After Dinner Conversation—February 2022 issue.

Discussion Questions

1. Everyone at the ad agency seems to agree that looking at old ads for ideas and inspiration is fine. Also, they all agree copying ads with minor changes to font and color are fine. What is the difference between finding inspiration from and plagiarizing another person's art?

2. Should Evan have told his firm the truth right after his advertisement was awarded a Gold? What is your calculation/reasoning that leads you to this conclusion?

3. Why can't the firm simply be honest and put on Evan's termination letter, "Fired at the request of a profitable client for doing something we wouldn't normally fire someone for, but we value keeping the client more than keeping a single employee?" Doesn't that also make the firm unethical?

4. Would you hire the newly fired Evan to work at your advertising agency? Why/why not? Would your answer be different if he was a more talented designer?

5. Can an action be unethical if it is the "industry practice?" Is it possible for there to be ethical employee behavior that nobody actually does in practice?

* * *

Pandora's Dreams

Peter Beaumont

* * *

Five years ago we opened Pandora's box. Blinded by hubris, we didn't foresee the problems that would arise. Only later did we realize our work would have such horrible implications, and as the story of Pandora goes, it's too late once the bad stuff gets out of the box. Now things are a mess and I guess we are to blame. You would be right to judge us harshly, and I won't hope for your forgiveness, but perhaps you might eventually understand how we got here and where we might end up if something isn't done.

I still remember the day well. It was early spring. A tang of vitality hung in the mild morning air as I climbed out of my car and walked slowly to the lab, weary from the late night and stuck in a loop of thinking I couldn't escape. Why wasn't it working? Where had we gone wrong? What had I missed?

We had been working late all week, sustained by a stubborn, almost desperate self-belief. We knew we were close. Close enough to believe the next day would be the breakthrough. Or the next. We just had to keep at it and ignore the poisonous doubt lurking in the long pauses between conversation; the doubt that it actually might not be possible to achieve.

None of us wanted to walk away from the years of work. From the years of sweet-talking potential investors and cajoling skittish board members. From the years of telling each other and anyone else who would listen that if we couldn't make the biggest advancement in neuroscience in decades, then no one could.

We had run the latest version of the program seven nights in a row without success. Each morning we had grimly accepted the disappointment and sent the volunteers on their way. Each morning our frustration accumulated like weeds choking a garden, and I wondered which of us might crack first under the pressure.

Then something changed.

On the eighth morning the result for two of the subjects was different. The quality was poor, and there was no sound, but irrefutably and quite remarkably we had finally succeeded in recording and playing back a human dream.

There was a reverent silence for five, ten seconds, then the room burst into life. People were shouting, laughing. Someone slapped my back. I stood rooted to the spot, eyes still focused on the wall-mounted screen in stunned disbelief. Someone called out to replay it, and as we watched again, the significance of what we had achieved began to sink in.

I still feel a flicker of the awe from that day. Like the small tremors that continue long after an earthquake has struck.

Looking back, I know we should have paused during

those first heady days to consider the implications of what we were doing, but if you can imagine the excitement we experienced that day then you might understand why we didn't. We had persevered and been rewarded, and were doubly determined to stay the course from there on in.

To say all the possible implications were unknowable is inexcusable, I know. Just as I know all we could think about on that day, and for many after, was the startling, beautiful things we could do with our discovery. And if we were honest – at least with ourselves – some of us were also imagining fame and glory. We were only human after all.

You won't be surprised to know that once we fixed the bugs in the system and moved to the full trial phase, the first participant was a rich entrepreneur. One of that infamous group rich enough to build private spacecraft and a boldness that could mesmerize millions with a grand vision of the future.

Some of the team weren't happy about blurring the boundaries between science and capitalism, but given our benefactor was prepared to donate a sizable portion of his wealth to the trial it was impossible to say no. And let's face it. Science doesn't happen unless someone pays the bills, and compared to the stifling bureaucracy of the university system we worked in, his proposition was beautiful in its simplicity. All we had to do was allow him to be the first to use it. Beyond that he wanted nothing, and in return he gave us more than enough money to make our dream project real. What reasonable person could refuse that?

So there we were. We had worked out how to record dreams and play them back. I was almost going to say play back at our leisure, but five years of viewing the confused, disturbing, even horrific creations of the unconscious mind has been as far from leisure as you could imagine.

The project was originally conceived with a noble intent. We had theorized that the roots of mental illness, trauma and certain cognitive disorders lay hidden somewhere within the deep, dark folds of the unconscious mind. Dreams were a manifestation of this little-understood function of the human brain, and we were confident that if we could capture and analyze them, we might be able to tease out the causes of these afflictions, and just possibly, find a cure.

There was so much we could have achieved, but – and I'm ashamed to say this now – we allowed commercial interests to override our therapeutic goal.

Once news got out that we could record and play back dreams, people clamored to get access to it. And those able to pay the hefty price were more than happy to do so.

Overnight, orbiting Earth as a space tourist dropped to number two on the must-do list of the mega-rich and would-be famous. After that there was, as they say, no holding back the tide.

With that, our research unit was transformed into a corporate entity, and in the eyes of some – ourselves included – we stopped being scientists and became salesmen. Soon the researchers and technicians were outnumbered by the marketers, lawyers, accountants and the quickly despised band of executives who cared only for profit and growth.

A year after that we made the next important breakthrough, improving the technology so that it could be housed in a portable unit and used by our clients at home. We had to install some seriously large computing hardware in our new facility to be able to handle all the incoming dream data, and then hire loads more technicians to keep it all running, but it's what the customers – and therefore the shareholders – wanted, so no one balked at it.

The units were clunky at first, and a little unreliable, but that was fixed in time. More problematic was some of the early client feedback. A number of people were confused and shocked by what they were confronted with, and a few couldn't handle it at all. We did our best to reassure them, sometimes cajoled them, and where necessary, directed them to a discreet counseling service to work through the more unpleasant stuff. The lawyers had also insisted we get all clients to sign an indemnity absolving us of any responsibility for harm should it occur, and a few clients had to be reminded of this as a last resort. Despite all this, enough clients continued on to tell their friends and social media followers about the miracle of their captured dreams – with perhaps some judicious self-editing in the telling – which fanned the flames of envy and drove enough demand on which to base a business.

Eventually, anybody prepared to pay the charges could sign up for a week, a month, even a year of recording, and have their dreams polished and sent back before the end of each day for them to view. It should have been a great success story. But then the problems began to emerge.

It didn't take long before people realized they could sell their dreams. Or worse, that recorded dreams could be stolen and sold on the black market for a good price if they were entertaining enough.

Humanity has always had a hankering to be entertained, and here was a new form just waiting to be exploited. Sexy, terrifying, disturbing, poignant, mystifying, thrilling: dreams offered it all, and there was always someone somewhere prepared to pay to watch it. More than one of our critics described our business as producing just another form of pornography.

Then came the more *entrepreneurial* activity. Someone worked out that here was a wonderful means by which to blackmail the rich and vulnerable. They would threaten to make public a stolen copy of a more *problematic* dream if the targeted victim failed to pay a significant sum of money. Needless to say, the willingness of victims to pay increased markedly after the blackmailers released the dream of one notable public figure who tried to call their bluff.

We couldn't work out how the dreams were being stolen. We tried beefing up system security, but to no avail. Much to my anger and disgust I eventually had to accept that at least one of our own staff was involved. It seemed that not only were the rich happy to pay for our unique service, but sometimes those wanting to be rich were prepared to break the rules to join them.

It's fair to say the clients weren't impressed. Most of them received sizable and discreet payments from the company for their trouble. All part of doing business, according to the company executives.

As troubling as this was, it was far from the worst of it.

The government took an interest in our system, seeing it as a potential tool in the fight against crime and terrorism. Why wait until someone is stupid enough to let slip their plans, or to act on them? Why not catch them in the act of dreaming about it and use it as preemptory evidence against them instead?

Now I've nothing against public safety, but using our

technology in this way leaves us in a difficult situation. Are we obliged to report any dreams that might be suggestive of criminal intent? What if poor old client X had watched a particularly violent film the night before, and then had a dream influenced by it? What if client Y had suffered an intense trauma and their unconscious mind played it over and over again in an attempt to make sense of it? Would these dreams be sufficient to warrant intervention by the authorities, and therefore require us to report them? And whose job would it be to try to interpret and justify the dreams as being a reliable indicator of criminality? Or for that matter, to explain how an unconscious desire will invariably lead to conscious action?

The libertarian lawyers and philosophers have had a field day with it so far. Dreams are private property they argue, and shouldn't be interfered with or used against someone, regardless of the circumstances. They decry the trampling of human rights and question the morality of this newfound omniscient justice.

And where might it end? There are rumors the government will soon mandate that everyone have a unit installed at home to record their dreams and transmit them to some government agency for monitoring. I'll leave it to your imagination as to what that might lead to next.

Perhaps I'm imagining the worst, but I'm not alone. There's a small but growing protest movement speaking out these days. Much of their effort is directed at the government, but not surprisingly, they have also taken aim at us. Online harassment of the company is now a daily occurrence, and I've read more than my fair share of nasty emails and social media posts directed at me.

They're mostly demanding the technology be banned,

claiming it's dangerous and that we don't know what we are doing. Worse are the suggestions that we are part of a government conspiracy which can only be fixed by violent revolutionary means.

Several of my colleagues left recently, spooked supposedly by the more unpleasant attacks. I heard one or two were offered considerable sums to work for dream recording outfits starting up in countries with less stringent regulatory controls.

So be it. I have no right to judge them. Others can.

The time of my own reckoning is now close.

Yesterday I dreamt I was standing in the vast processing vault beneath our lab that houses the row after row of computer servers. In the dream I walked over to a terminal, logged in, then hesitated as I looked around at the quietly humming machines that store a million dreams and more. I knew what I had to do, but what person wouldn't pause at the thought of destroying their own creation?

Then cold certainty took over and I entered the command, ignored the alert that came up, and re-entered it. A moment passed, and then it was done. The servers powered down and left me sitting in an eerily silent space. I felt a pang of sadness, followed by a growing sense of dread, then the dream ended.

That was yesterday morning.

Today I sit in my apartment under house arrest, awaiting the arrival of the authorities. No reason was given in the notification, but I know my dream must have been the cause.

I should have known my dreams would be monitored when I recorded them. I had found watching them a strangely cathartic experience after focusing intently on those of others. Naively, I overlooked the prospect of the company and the government being interested in them as well.

Now I wait to be judged by some government inquisitor, and, I suppose, by you in time.

I wonder what advice Oppenheimer would have for me if he were here today.

In moments of despondent clarity I have wondered if we were meant to fully know our dreams; whether we opened a door to the unconscious world that was never meant to be opened. Perhaps we should just accept the notion that dreams serve a useful purpose and leave it at that. To accept that there are some things that will and should remain unknowable. After all, do we really want to confront the proposition that part of our brain is working autonomously, almost like a separate mind of its own? Based on some of my own dreams it seems my unconscious mind is more than ready to cast harsh judgment on me for my role in this.

Enough for now. There's little hope for me, but perhaps it's not too late for someone else to act. For someone to not just protest against the sinister future we are hurtling towards, but to lead a movement to prevent it. For someone brave enough to try to do what Pandora could not; to put the evils of the world back inside the box.

* * *

This story first appeared in the After Dinner Conversation—February 2021 issue.

Discussion Questions

1. If you could buy, and watch, the dreams of others, would you do it? Why or why not?
2. Would you allow your own dreams to be recorded? Would you allow them to be sold, or watched by others? What do you think our dreams reveal?
3. If you could buy and watch (*or have*) a particular dream, what topics or stories would you want to try out?
4. Do you think people who have (*or want to buy*) violent or deviant dreams are (*or will become*) violent or deviant people? Do you think dreams should be used to provide cause for believing a future crime will take place?
5. Do you think there are areas of scientific research, like atomic bombs, viruses, human cloning, or dream recording, that should be banned from ever being researched?

* * *

Cicada

Ishan Dylan

* * *

Dr. Kamilah Zhang failed to turn up for her eight o'clock physics lecture on a cold Tuesday morning, leaving her students to grumble about *unprofessional conduct*. One student, a philosophy major, even went so far as to suggest — *unethical*.

By nine o'clock, nobody on the planet was still talking about professionalism.

* * *

In the video, Dr. Zhang sat next to a bookshelf. Behind her was a sixteenth-century poster of the solar system. She wore a lab coat over a dark blouse and a strand of pearls.

"It's done."

She pushed ahead without pausing for the words to land, seemingly unaware of their momentousness. "I don't just mean proof that it's possible. The technology for interstellar travel is complete. It's ours. Today."

* * *

But we couldn't make that the headline, of course. Dr. Zhang hadn't published her calculations. We couldn't risk our credibility. Then again—as multiple coworkers vented to me—Dr. Zhang *was* a credible source. It was frustrating. We were about to get beaten to history by the grocery store tabloid aisle.

After an hour of pitches and one shattered coffee mug, the managing editor settled on my draft: *Prototype for Interstellar Travel Complete, Says Renowned Physicist.*

It was honest. Not too flashy. Journalists aren't supposed to make promises we can't support. Our responsibility is to the truth, not dreams. The public deserves the truth.

* * *

Kids deserve to dream.

"When we go to space, where do you want to visit first?" Jade tugged the sheets to her chin.

I pretended to think. "Let's go to Titan. Surface oceans and fourteen percent gravity. The perfect vacation spot."

That earned me the eye roll I was expecting. "You can't surf on Titan, Dad. They're hydrocarbon lakes, not oceans. It's not dense enough. You'd just sink."

"Oh. Silly me." Outer space was one topic I did not have to feign any ignorance on. "What about you?"

"I can't tell you," her face was deadly serious, "because I'm going to an undiscovered planet. I think I'll name it *Shiva.*"

"Wow. You've got this all figured out, haven't you?"

"Maybe not the name. But all the other planets are named after Roman gods, and that's not very fair."

"How about *Ma'at*," I offered, "the goddess of truth and justice."

Jade looked at me pityingly, like I was the child who

needed explaining to. "But I already *have* a backup name," she insisted, "Planet Bobby."

Bobby was her pet hamster's name.

I chuckled and kissed her forehead. "I'm sure you can discover two planets, sunshine."

* * *

"She's got nothing!" my boss roared. "Nada! Zilch!"

"We didn't *say* she had anything," I massaged my temples, "just that she *claimed* to have something. I'll report the leak, okay...?"

I stared at the blank document for long enough that my coffee got cold. Finally, I managed to type a headline. *NASA Leak Proves Interstellar Travel Claims Fraudulent.* I stared at the words until they were just black shapes on a screen. Then I made a correction. *NASA Leak Suggests...*

Next, there was the question of why she did it. Everyone at work had their own theory. It fell to me to copyedit them into something usable. I came across more than one contemporary paraphrase of "female hysteria."

* * *

With Jade at school, the house was empty. I used to walk the dog when I needed to get outside. But Scout was dead. I wandered down the sidewalk without an excuse. That year, it was easy to pick out the newly gentrified streets. I only had to look for which trees weren't crawling with cicadas, trees that hadn't been here seventeen years ago.

I watched the tiny marvels squirm from the mulch. *Beautiful things from the earth as well.* The nymphs emerge with vigor. Only a month to breed, only a month, breed breed breed, they thought. *They don't need to know about the stars.*

* * *

April 13th. It would go down in history as the day when... well, *April 13th* happened. No explanation needed. *July 4th. September 11th. April 13th.*

"It's a fake. It's a hack, or a... photo-chop or something."

"Photoshop."

"Whatever. It's a hoax. Do *not* report on this."

I looked back at my monitor, at the same compressed JPEG that was probably loaded on every screen in the world. Rolling red hills. A landscape that, by appearances, could have been from Earth, but of course, that would be impossible. Visible plainly in the Martian soil, footprints spelled a phrase now overwhelming the servers of Google Translate: *Quod erat demonstrandum.* Translation: *believe me now?*

* * *

The FBI found her on a ranch in Wyoming. No spaceship, no magic gateway. Just her, a woman in a lab coat. A podcaster started a theory that Dr. Zhang somehow used the Mars rover itself to write the message—*She's some kind of genius, isn't she? Like, a hacker genius?* The accusation trended for several hours until the internet collectively realized that rovers don't have feet.

It was a striking front-page photo. A pile of shredded paper and scorched motherboards. During interrogation, reportedly, Dr. Zhang smugly informed the investigators that there was still one type of memory drive their technology could not search.

But not even the constraints of reality can stop a congressional subpoena. Congress opened an investigation into Dr. Zhang's "destruction of government property" under Title 18, US Code § 1361, and article eight of the Outer Space Treaty.

That's what I had to write. The facts. If you really wanted to know what Kamilah Zhang was on trial for, you just had to check social media. Everyone was arguing the same question.

If she had the technology, why didn't she share it?

People fell into three camps. The first declared the April 13th phenomenon a hoax. The second, that Dr. Zhang was extorting the US government. The third camp declared everything else, ranging from something about alien body snatchers to the sinister machinations of a particular ex-secretary of state.

There was really no point in theorizing. You could just wait for the Congressional Record to release their transcripts.

* * *

The Senate Subcommittee on Commerce, Justice, Science, and Related Agencies was ready to convene the moment Kamilah Zhang touched down in Washington. Congress even came out of recess for the occasion. Senator Huxley presided.

When it came time for her to speak, Kamilah Zhang leaned almost imperceptibly closer to the microphone. "The data from my laboratory are considered records. I made the decision not to refer them to the Aeronautics and Space Administration."

"So you willfully disregarded your duty," Senator Huxley continued, "your... *sacred* duty, which you swore to uphold—"

"That's where we disagree," Dr. Zhang interrupted. "Oppenheimer fulfilled his duty on paper, but what about his duty to the world? Of course," she said, beginning to lean away from the microphone, "of course, he owed his superiors answers. But he could have drawn out the search. Keep them looking into heavy water, for example... buy time for a peaceful end."

A remarkably optimistic view. But that wasn't what Senator Huxley took issue with.

"Destroying government records is treason."

"Please. Some decorum," Senator Hart spoke up. Blue pantsuit. Third in line for the Democratic nomination. "Look, Dr. Zhang. I understand. Here you are," she emphasized with a squint, "with the power to change history."

"I don't want to be Oppenheimer—"

"—and responsibility can be awfully stressful—"

"—I want to be Frederick Banting."

A pause of confusion turned into real silence as Dr. Zhang drew herself up. "Banting. The man who sold the patent of insulin for one dollar, who ensured that his research would save lives rather than generate profit."

"Then follow his example," Senator Hart insisted, "share your research."

"Insulin today costs $360.25 per month," Dr. Zhang replied. "This economy didn't deserve Banting's trust. It will have to earn mine."

"Dr. Zhang," Senator Huxley interjected, "have you had any affiliation with the Communist Party of China?"

"Mister Senator, I think I've made very clear my position on any such profit-driven entities." Kamilah wouldn't let him goad her into producing any sound bites. "Look. I am willing to disclose some details from my research. They are necessary details to understand my decision."

The room quieted.

"The technology that I have developed can transport

matter anywhere in the universe. Senator Hart, imagine what could be done with that kind of capability..."

"We could have clean energy, better waste management—"

"I agree. We could have benefits for all mankind, which is to say—not profits. But is that what Amazon and Exxon-Mobil will think of, Senator? How will you respond when corporations start hosting off-world fulfillment centers far, far away from US jurisdiction?"

The Congressional Record doesn't include air quotes in its transcripts. You'll have to guess where she put them.

"The federal government exists to regulate private industry, Dr. Zhang," Senator Hart said. "It exists to address these very concerns."

"With all due respect, Senator. The purpose of a machine is what we use it for."

* * *

When the FBI took Dr. Zhang into custody, the editorial board called it an "unprecedented breach of judicial norms." They imprisoned her so that she couldn't give her discovery to any foreign governments. That's what we were saying.

I was assigned to write a piece reminding everyone to be very concerned about precedents. Even if you didn't agree with Dr. Zhang, her civil liberties were our own.

It needed to be said.

I would leave it for someone else to say. I decided to call out of work.

* * *

I was on another walk when I heard something hiss beneath me. A cicada helpless on the concrete, its broken legs waggling in the air.

Normally, I'd squash it. Call it a mercy killing. I stared down at the concrete.

We didn't have to be trapped here. There was someone who could help us. *Someone too busy arguing with millionaires on C-SPAN*, I fumed.

The newsroom and the editorial board hadn't been on speaking terms since the announcement. But it was the only thing I had the energy to write.

OPINION: Kamilah Zhang Thinks Her Politics Are the Center of the Universe. She's Wrong.

* * *

I was expecting my coworkers to be angry. It was only fair. Who knew how many hate messages had been lobbed at them because of what I wrote?

What I wasn't expecting was for my boss to walk in with a buddy-buddy smile plastered across his face. I furrowed my brow.

"*Great* timing. Really had your finger on the pulse for this one."

I didn't understand his sarcasm until he dropped an early draft of today's front page on my desk.

Dr. Kamilah Zhang Dead of Apparent Suicide in Federal Custody.

"Good luck out there, Krish. You'll need it."

* * *

Someone had to drive Jade to school. I tried to ignore the scathing looks. A few days ago, all these PTA parents in their smart watches and yoga pants had silently agreed with me. But that wouldn't show up if you googled their names. Not like my op-ed.

I had it out for her all along. That's what social media thought. Why else had I refused to report on Dr. Zhang between the first announcement and her death?

I started taking my walks late at night when the streets were empty. I slept while Jade was at school. I didn't have to worry about work since quitting, but I still couldn't escape the endless theorizing of my coworkers.

If they couldn't have the technology, nobody could. So they killed her.

No, they're dissecting her brain to figure it out. That's why we haven't seen the body.

I couldn't speculate. Only one question consumed my nightly walks.

Why did she tell us if she knew we couldn't meet her demands?

Guilt gnawed at me. A woman was dead, and I was mourning her research.

* * *

"What's that?" I pointed at the piece of poster board in Jade's hands as she climbed into the backseat of the minivan.

She turned it around. *Galileo* was written in bubble letters across the top.

"Nice! Are you gonna study space someday, like he did...?"

"Maybe," she replied glumly. "Ms. Kleinman said it was too late to change my presentation topic."

"Oh. Okay."

* * *

Once Jade was in bed, I flipped open my laptop.

It was just a school project. But it reminded me of something that I couldn't name. It was on the tip of my tongue.

My fingers hovered over the keyboard. I typed the only thing that ever crossed my mind when it was otherwise blank.

Kamilah Zhang.

42,800,000 results. My cursor hovered over the video thumbnail.

Click.

"It's done," her voice came through the speakers.

Click. Muted.

I didn't want to listen, to fool myself into thinking she was there and talking to me. That would mean I could apologize. I looked at the wall behind her. Something had been strange about the poster. Now I saw what. Earth was at the center, surrounded by concentric gold rings.

Galileo would go down in history for defending heliocentrism until he died, imprisoned for heresy. Religion versus science. The passion of Christ versus the passion for truth. Martyr versus martyr. I stared at the poster behind Dr. Zhang.

It was a message. A time capsule.

Everyone liked to imagine that they would side with Galileo. Especially journalists. After all, our first duty was to truth, even if we don't like where it leads. Or the enemies it leads us to.

* * *

Jade asked if she could stay up past her bedtime to join me on my nightly walk.

"Wait up!" she called out a few meters behind me. She was on her hands and knees, parsing through the wet grass.

"What are you doing?"

"Looking for bugs. New ones. There could be a brand-new kind of bug right here! I read that over eight hundred insect species are discovered every year."

I didn't even think about correcting her. Kids deserve to dream. I nodded along, half-listening.

"Bugs bugs bugs bugs bugs."

I stared at the tree trunks, covered with the translucent, amber carapaces where cicadas had crawled from their exoskeletons.

I stared at the empty husks and frowned. They leave behind their old bodies. They do not hold onto old weight to fly...

We never saw her body.

* * *

This story first appeared in the After Dinner Conversation—August 2023 issue.

Discussion Questions

1. The narrator (*Krish*) says, "Everyone liked to imagine that they would side with Galileo." What does this mean? Why would people side against new science? Why might you side with, or against, Galileo (*or Dr. Zhang*)?

2. What do you think are the ramifications of Dr. Zhang's discovery, assuming it is true? Do you think it would be a net positive, or negative, for humanity?

3. Why do you think Dr. Zhang wanted to prove her discovery to the world only to deny providing it? If you were in her situation, what would you do? Do you think an inventor who withholds world-changing technology deserves civil liberties, or do the needs of the many outweigh one individual's liberties?

4. If you had a world-changing discovery that you wanted to guarantee would get out into the world in the most nonprofit-driven way, how would you do it? Under what, if any, circumstances should a world-changing discovery be driven by profit motives?

5. What do you think happened to Dr. Zhang?

* * *

Claim

Fiona Ennis

* * *

In the tiny room that's used as a staff canteen in Halden Insurance, you take two Ryvita out for your lunch, snap one in half, then put the bigger half back in your lunchbox. Maura licks the egg mayonnaise that's spilling out of her sandwich as she watches you slice a tomato. She'll probably make some comment about you being too thin again. Her dark blonde fringe, sprayed to the last, stands up straight over her forehead, and you can see where the teeth of the comb were pulled through the strands. The rest of her hair is backcombed. She thinks she looks like one of the Bangles or something. The last time she gave you a lift home when it was raining, she played 'Manic Monday' and then fast-forwarded the tape to 'Walk like an Egyptian', doing the hand actions when she stopped at the traffic lights. Seán, your boss, asked her last week to tone down the hair a bit, look more professional when she's talking to clients, not that her hair bothered him as such, he'd said, but she had to think of the company image. Most days she slicks her hair back with that wet look gel, but not today, as she's heading out for drinks after work. Not that he'll say anything. She'll probably end up in Club Tempo after. It's free in for women on Thursdays. Ladies' Night. She'll be dying in the morning again.

The kettle shudders on the countertop and clicks just as Seán walks in. His jacket is hanging off him. You don't know why he always carries a copy of *The Irish Times* to the canteen each day. He never ends up reading it.

He nods at you. 'The usual?'

'Yep. Thanks.'

He puts a teaspoon of coffee into the red mug and another into his special mug.

Maura points a frosted pink nail at your plate. 'Don't know how you can be full on one and a half Ryvita. Still, it's a quarter more than you had yesterday, isn't it, Niamh? And Seán, since you're asking, I'll have a cuppa too.'

He opens the box of tea and throws a bag in the yellow mug with the chip off the side. 'Sure, that's why she's so lovely and thin, isn't it?'

Maura raises her tadpole eyebrows.

He smiles at you, and his eyes graze over your legs. You pull at your pencil skirt a bit.

Then he says, 'Did you know Greta Garbo used to insure her legs for millions?'

Maura puts down the crust of her sandwich and takes out a Penguin bar. 'Yeah, I heard Tina Turner does that. Dunno if it's true. Imagine if we got a call from someone around here asking for that?'

He brings over the coffee. When Maura looks at him, he goes back for her tea.

As he sits down beside you, you move your chair and say, 'Imagine the actuaries working out that one?'

He laughs. 'Ah, I don't think the premiums would be too high somehow.'

Maura is in the bathroom, fixing up her makeup before she hits the pub. The office phone rings. It's ten to five. Typical. This had better not hold you up. Your stomach is growling, and you have to do your aerobics video before dinner.

You say, 'Hello, Halden Insurance. Niamh speaking. How may I help you?'

A woman's voice says, 'Ah, Niamh. Glad I got you before closing. It's Margaret, the bishop's secretary.'

'What can I do for you, Margaret?' The diocese is a huge account. This could take ages.

'Well, we're trying to insure against all sorts of risks. There are a lot of people against the Church these days.'

'Dreadful, isn't it?' You're glad she doesn't know you voted in favor of legalizing divorce last year, not that the referendum passed. Seán had told Maura not to be attending those pro-divorce protests in town, in case it got back. He doesn't know she headed off on the bus to that rally in Dublin, bringing all the flyers with her that she'd copied on the office machine.

Margaret's voice is barely loud enough to hear. 'People are making all sorts of allegations against a few of the priests.'

'Imagine, after they've given up their lives for the Church.'

'We'll have to take out some unusual cover, in the interests of the diocese, and the priests too, of course.'

'Right. What kind of policy, Margaret?' Your shoe is

chafing your right heel, and you slip your shoe off and dangle it from your toes.

'One that protects the diocese against liability arising from sexual abuse of children by priests.'

'Excuse me?' Your shoe falls to the floor.

'Is there a problem?'

'No, no, of course not.'

You knock on Seán's office door. It's after five, but he always works late.

'Come in.' He's sitting at his desk and smiles when you enter. 'Shouldn't you have gone home by now? I'm working you too hard.'

'Pay rise?'

He lets out a breath through his teeth. 'Yeah, right. Feels like the economy is never going to pick up.'

'I need to talk to you about something.'

He indicates for you to take a seat, then sits back in his chair and rakes his fingers through his hair.

You sit and pull your skirt over your knees. 'I just got a call from Margaret, the bishop's secretary.'

'Oh yeah?'

How are you going to put this? 'She was inquiring about a policy to insure the diocese against liability for sexual abuse of children by priests.'

'What's that now?' He sits forward and puts his hands on the desk.

'A policy to protect against liability for sex abuse of children by priests.'

'Right, right.' He rubs his forehead.

'So, what do we do?'

'Do?'

'Like report it?'

He taps his pen on the desk, then stares at it for a moment. 'No, we won't be doing that.'

'They could be near kids.'

'Niamh, we protect against liability. Just because we insure a house against fire, doesn't mean the house will go on fire. This is just protection in case claims are made. Insurance 101.'

'You don't believe that.'

'I do. Anyway, this is confidential. You're not to mention it to anyone.'

He cannot be serious.

He says, 'I mean it, Niamh.'

'I have to.'

His neck is mottled. 'You can't cast aspersions on people's characters, least of all on our clients. You'd better keep it to yourself.' Then he opens a desk drawer. 'I've a stack of CVs here from girls just like you. You'd have no prospects on the dole queue. You know yourself factories are closing up and down the country.'

You watch as he closes the drawer. It feels like it happens so slowly.

Then he looks at you, like really looks at you. 'Niamh, I don't want to lose you. Just do the paperwork tomorrow; there's a good girl. But keep any documents relating to it out of Maura's sight. You know what she's like.'

You get up from the chair and close the door behind you.

After the forty-minute walk home from work, you let

yourself into your bedsit. You hate waking up in the same room as your fridge and TV, and the rent is pretty high considering the flowery wallpaper is peeling, and the carpet is lifting away from the skirting board. A loud grumble comes from your stomach, but you've always been like that, wanting to eat because something's eating you. You preheat the oven, change into your t-shirt and tracksuit pants and rewind your Jane Fonda video. This should take your mind off things. By the time the video is over, your dinner should be ready. You take a Lean Cuisine Sweet and Sour Chicken out of the freezer. At least you don't need a microwave for this flavor, or for the Chicken Fried Rice one, even though the rice sometimes gets hard in the oven and tastes like little pellets. Still, at least you know what's in them: 300 calories, so two thirds of it today = 200 calories. You've learned not to leave the third you don't want on your plate. Well, it's not that you don't want it, but you always put it in the bin before you even sit down. You peel off the film, pop it out of the container and put it in the oven. Then you move the tiny table and chair nearer your bed so you can do your workout.

You do your waist-whittlers, and even though you're sweating and trying to concentrate on the exercises, you keep replaying that conversation with Seán. Maura would have stood up to him. And she would have done something already. Why are you so useless? Utterly useless. You put your mat on the carpet to do your inner thigh exercises. You hate these. You do two, then you stop doing them and just lie there, even though Jane is being really encouraging on the TV. You stare at the big brown stain on the ceiling, just near the light, then get up and turn off the video, not even noting where you were on the tape.

You've never stopped it partway through before.

When your dinner is ready you sit down, don't even bother scraping off the third you don't usually eat. You plow through it, rather than your usual slow mouthfuls, and when you've finished, you can feel it just sit there. You go into your bathroom, bend over the toilet bowl and retch. It's been a long time since you've done this, you've been so good at not doing it, so good at controlling everything that goes in so that you don't have to do this anymore, but your body remembers what to do. You don't even need to stick two fingers in your throat, like you used to when you started doing this back when you were twelve. The food just comes up your throat and plops out, the curry, mixed with acid, burning your throat. Lumps of chicken come up too. Grains of rice float in the bottom of the bowl. When no more will come up, you sit on the lino in front of the sink, crying, your arms around your legs. Not this again. You've been so good for so long. You can't go back to this.

* * *

Every day, while you sat on the primary school bus, staring at the fields go by, Leanne from your class would get onto you again about being fat, calling you Titanic and stuff, and who was she to talk? As if she had the perfect body or something. The last time she fell out with her two best friends, Neasa and Cara, they told everyone she stuffed her bra with tissues. Not that they were all that either: Cara had one blue eye and one brown eye, and Neasa's hair was always greasy. They weren't too bad to you though, didn't really call you names, but they laughed along with Leanne just the same. The day before you'd started making yourself sick after eating, Leanne had sat behind you on the bus and called you names, while you'd stared at the gloop in the corner of the black rubber around the window. David Nolan, who you had fancied all year, wasn't in the backseat where he usually sat. You'd got a seat near the front, and David had sat opposite and smiled at you. You hadn't imagined that. He'd been looking at you in class for the past few weeks, but on the bus that day, when Leanne started calling you Fatso really loudly, he'd got up and walked to the backseat, to the rest of the cool sixth class crowd, who picked old cigarette butts off the ground that were there from the town runs and smoked them.

Your cheeks were burning. You didn't want to go on like this anymore, wearing an enormous skirt with an elasticated waist. Your mum was always on at you about your weight, and even your auntie, who usually nudged her to stop, kept telling you how she had lost loads of weight by walking every day, so you decided to get off the bus early and walk a good part of the way home. Alan, the bus driver, could drop you at the sign that said three miles to your townland. That would be a good start. Your stop was the last one on the journey home every day. Leanne's stop was second last, and her house looked rundown. Her mum had run off with someone; everyone knew that, even though she said her mum was modeling in Paris. Every day, for the last part of the journey, when everyone except you and Leanne had left the bus, Alan, the driver, asked her to sit in the front seat and chat to him. He was in his thirties, which seemed ancient back then. He was always kind to you though.

When you reached the sign for your townland, before he'd called Leanne up to talk to him, you'd said, 'Can you let me off here?'

He'd said, 'Why?'

'I want the exercise.'

'Won't your mum be worried about you?'

'She won't be home until half five anyway.'

He'd stopped the bus and opened the door. 'Pop out so. And Niamh, don't let that name-calling get to you. They're only jealous because you've a pretty face.'

You'd looked at your feet as you'd walked down the steps. 'Thanks.'

The bus had lurched forward and drove out the road where there were no houses for ages. You'd adjusted your schoolbag on your back. It was a pity you hadn't had P.E. that day; you would have had your runners with you instead of your hard patent shoes.

The next morning when you got off the bus, Neasa and Cara stopped you. Leanne was standing over by the school gate. They nodded at you to wait with them until everyone else had gone. Class wouldn't start for another fifteen minutes.

Neasa said, 'We need you to come with us to Mrs. Crawford and tell her what that bus driver has been doing.'

You put your schoolbag on the ground for a minute. Your shoulders still hurt from carrying it the day before. 'What do you mean?'

'Leanne says he's always looking at her and getting her to come up and talk to him after everyone has gone. Yesterday, after you got off the bus early, he did stuff to her.'

'What kind of stuff?'

Neasa moved a bit nearer. 'He was touching her.'

You looked over at Leanne, leaning against the gate. 'She's lying.'

Cara said, 'What?'

'He's never called her up to talk to him. And I didn't get off the bus early. Why would I do that?'

Neasa pushed her fringe back from her face. 'Why would she lie?'

'She stuffs her bra with tissues. And she said her mum is a model in Paris. How can you believe a word she says?'

They looked over at her, then at each other.

Neasa said, 'Glad we talked to you. We could have got in a heap of trouble over this.' Then she walked up to Leanne and kicked some gravel at her. 'You're a dirty liar.'

That evening, even though you'd brought your runners with you, you didn't get off the bus early to walk home. But after everyone else had gone, you watched how Alan looked at Leanne in the mirror, and felt guilt wriggle its way through you and take hold. That evening after your mum served you chicken and veg, you went to the bathroom and put your fingers down your throat.

* * *

It's after lunch, and Maura has perked up a bit. She was hungover all morning and put her head down on her desk a few times, but after a Tayto sandwich and some Fanta, she's coming back to herself.

Seán's door is closed, but she keeps her voice low. 'I'm never drinking again. I mean it this time.'

You say, 'Yeah, right.'

'Anyway, what's up with himself? He barely said a word at lunchtime, not that I'm complaining.'

'Dunno.' You've finished working on the policy for Margaret, and the documents are in an envelope on your desk, ready to post, but you can't bring yourself to seal the envelope.

Maura looks at you. 'You're very quiet today. Why'd you stay on after I left at five? You're usually out of here like a hot snot.'

'Just had to talk to him about something.'

She comes over. 'Hope he didn't try it on. I've seen the way he gawps at you. I'm here if you want to tell me anything.'

You look at her for what feels like a whole minute. Then you pick up the envelope containing the policy and feel your fingers draw out the documents.

'I mean it,' she says. 'I can stand up to him.'

You slide the documents back in and put the envelope down. 'No, everything's okay, Maura.'

'You don't look like it is.'

'Don't worry. I'm fine. Thanks though.'

'If you're sure.' She goes back to her desk. 'I could do with some air. I'm off to post some documents. Have you got anything to go there?'

'Yep.'

You seal the envelope, hand it to her, and she walks out the door. You almost run after her, but instead, you go to the bathroom, pressing your forehead against the door. Then you lean over the toilet, and when you vomit, only a small piece of Ryvita comes up. It won't flush away.

* * *

This story first appeared in the After Dinner Conversation—August 2021 issue.

Discussion Questions

1. If you worked for an insurance company, would you be willing to insure a diocese against sexual abuse allegations? Are there some things you shouldn't be able to buy insurance against?

2. The narrator lied for the bus driver because she knew it would hurt the story of her school bully. Given the various factors, how do you judge the narrator for her actions?

3. The narrator's boss implies he would fire her for the ethical issues she has against insuring the church against sexual abuse charges. What, if anything, should the narrator have done in response to the threat, and why?

4. What exactly are the mental health issues the narrator has, and what would be the best steps/realizations for her to move forward to being a healthier individual?

5. Are there any additional questions you would want to ask before issuing sexual assault insurance for the church? What answers would permit, or preclude, you from issuing the insurance?

* * *

Thorn

Erik Fatemi

* * *

Joseph was never anyone I had to worry about. Joseph was a nobody. He did his work, went home to his family. That's as far as his ambitions went. If you needed someone to build a door, fix a stone wall—odd jobs like that—and you didn't have much money, you hired Joseph. He had his regulars, but not enough to cut into my business. Most of the time, verily, I forgot he even existed. So, no, Joseph wasn't my problem. My problem was his boy. I just didn't see it coming.

The first sign came about ten years ago. I was walking through the market, and, lo, there was Philip, the son of Matthias, in his usual stall, chattering nonstop to everyone who passed by. The finest pottery in town! The lowest prices! But I wasn't interested in his bowls and platters. My eyes went straight to two new cedar stools that he'd set out for customers. The seats, rectangular and contoured, were unlike any I'd seen before in Sepphoris. I'd already taken over most of the labor in town, and none of my people were capable of such craftsmanship. This was Temple-quality work. Whoever built these stools wouldn't be selling to potters for long. He'd go where the money was, to a better clientele. My clientele. I'd seen it before. In fact, I'd done the same thing myself when I was breaking into the business.

I needed to find out who made these stools.

Philip fussed over me when he saw me coming, and I took a seat. I'm tall, nearly four cubits, and I eat well. Most stools would prefer a lighter load, but this one supported me easily. I picked up an oil lamp from among his wares and pretended to examine it.

"Martha will love it," Philip said. He listed its many virtues in great detail and quoted a price we both knew was too high. He also knew I'd pay it, because I could.

I considered the offer, then rapped my knuckles on the empty stool next to me. "Not bad. Where'd you get them?"

Philip stammered, nervous he was about to lose a sale. "You know I always buy from you, Timothy. But—"

I smiled and held up my hand. "Just curious."

When he said Joseph, the son of Jacob, I made him repeat it. Impossible. Where did Joseph learn how to make stools like this?

* * *

James arrived at my house early the next morning, as usual, to review my affairs for the day. Sepphoris was booming, and it was a good time to be in construction. I'd known James since school, but we were never what you'd call friends. Other boys mocked him and called him James the Lesser because he was the smallest of the three Jameses in our class and as meek as a lamb. But I tolerated him. He followed me around, hanging on my every word, and that came in handy sometimes—as was still true all these years later. I paid him well, but he lived in a simple home and dressed plainly. He wasn't married and seemed to have no interests other than serving as my steward and doing whatever I asked of him. Today, that meant visiting Joseph's workshop, an hour and a half's walk to the south, to see if he had hired anyone or was still working by himself.

When James returned that afternoon, he said Joseph was alone, except for his son.

"Was the boy doing anything?" I asked. "Or just watching?"

James checked his writing tablet before answering. He took notes on everything. "He hammered some nails, but that was all."

In hindsight, I should have put Joseph out of business then and there. It would have saved me a lot of trouble later. But I let it go. I was expanding into Cana at the time, so I was often on the road. And Martha was with child—John, my firstborn son—and I was building a new home (the one before where we now live). I had bigger things to think about than a few stools.

Years passed, and my business continued to flourish. The Romans hired me to build a stable in Capernaum, and that opened up a multitude of new opportunities for me— everything from crosses to courthouses. My laborers grumbled about working for Romans, but I had no interest in politics. Silver was silver.

Life was just as good at home. Martha gave birth to our daughter, Elizabeth, and my second son, Luke. I bought land on the highest hill in Sepphoris and built a mansion almost worthy of Solomon, with eight rooms, mosaic floors, and indoor baths.

As James said, the greatest builder in Galilee should have the finest house. Same for the garden. I filled it with lilies and roses and all manner of fruits: figs, dates, pomegranates, apples. And olives, of course. I hired a servant to care for it full-time. Maybe my father used to tend a garden like mine. I would have enjoyed ordering him around.

So I had little reason to think about Joseph. I bumped into him occasionally if he had a job here in town, but we rarely spoke. Then James told me one morning that Joseph had died. He'd been sick for a long time—some sort of palsy.

I stopped listening. Construction on a wall I was building in Magdala was running behind schedule, and I couldn't afford any more delays.

"His son is taking over his shop," James said.

This made me pause. He was just one carpenter in a lowly village, but you could never be too careful. "Keep an eye on him," I said.

* * *

Then it came to pass that James said he needed to show me something at the synagogue. I hadn't stepped foot inside it in months and didn't plan on returning until the next high holiday. I'd suffered through enough services as a boy, thanks to my father. He earned practically nothing as a gardener, but every week he'd tithe a fifth of his wages—double what the scriptures required. Every night when we weren't at the synagogue, he'd read aloud from the Torah to my brothers and me while my mother mended holes in our threadbare tunics. So I'd had my fill of religion and the poverty that came with it. If my competitors wanted to waste their time at services, good for them. They'd be working for me soon anyway.

The synagogue was badly in need of repair; no doubt the priests were pocketing the tithes for themselves. The roof leaked, the benches wobbled, and the holy ark—a cabinet built into a recess in the wall that held the Torah scrolls—was on the verge of falling apart. Even a nonbeliever like myself found it embarrassing. If it had been up to me, I'd have torn the whole structure down and rebuilt it. But as soon as James brought me inside, I knew what he wanted me to see. The ark had been replaced, and the new one was astonishing.

It had two doors that opened from the center, like the old one, and was the same size as the original. But the craftsmanship was flawless. I reached out to touch it, then drew short. There was something strange about it—almost as if it had been there forever, and the synagogue constructed around it.

"Joseph's son," James said. "He donated it."

So that was my second sign. I knew then that I'd been right about Philip's stools: Joseph hadn't built them after all. But I never guessed it was his boy. Where'd he been hiding all these years? Waiting for Joseph to die? It didn't make sense. But whatever his reason for lying low in the past, he must have cast it aside. If you were an up-and-coming carpenter and wanted to show off your talent, the synagogue was the place to do it. I had to admit, it was a cunning move. I should have thought of it myself.

If I didn't act quickly, this boy could be a thorn in my side for many years to come.

* * *

With his short legs, James took three steps for every two of mine. "This way," he said, pointing left as we entered the village.

I'd been to Nazareth many times, most recently for a cousin's wedding. I could see why Joseph liked it here: nothing but average people, living unexceptional lives. Salt of the earth, the rabbis called them. The sooner I could leave, the better.

I smelled bread baking in an oven as we passed a communal kitchen. All these little villages had them; each one served several families. Near the entrance, an old blind man sat with his back to the trunk of an olive tree. When he heard us approaching, he started banging his cup with a stick, begging for money. We ignored him, and James turned right, proceeded about fifty cubits, then stopped in front of a modest workshop. Tools were arranged neatly on a bench. A table displayed a few items for sale: a small wooden box, a carved horse, some household utensils.

Joseph's son was unloading a cypress bough from a wagon when we arrived, so he didn't notice us at first. He was no more than thirty, medium build, and unremarkable in every way. Not ugly, but not handsome, either. His commonness disappointed me. This was the master carpenter? I wondered if James had directed me to the wrong man until, lo, he swung his axe into the limb and cleaved it in half. And I mean exactly in half. He laid the two pieces side by side; neither was a hair longer than the other.

"You have great talent," I said.

He looked up, and I had the feeling he already knew me. But then, most laborers in Galilee would have recognized Timothy the builder. He struck twice again with his axe, and now there were four pieces, all the same length. "My father taught me well," he said.

"No offense to Joseph. He was a diligent worker and a

righteous man. But you're twice the carpenter that he ever was."

He set one of the four pieces on a table and, selecting an adze from his collection of tools, began stripping away the bark. He worked deliberately, but no motion was wasted.

"A man with your skill could do very well for himself if the right opportunity came along," I said. Again, no answer. My heart began to harden. If he truly recognized me, then he knew I deserved respect.

My thoughts were interrupted by two young men passing by. One grabbed his companion by the arm, and they stopped to talk. The first man said he'd been a good son. He worked hard and looked after his father—not like his older brother, who'd demanded his inheritance, squandered all his money on wine and whores, then came crawling back, begging for mercy.

Joseph's son paused to listen as the young man raised his voice. His father gave his brother a feast! He served him a fatted calf! Why should he have to settle for scraps while his good-for-nothing brother stuffed his belly?

The men moved on, and Joseph's son returned to his adze, but the story gave me an idea.

"Your father blessed you with something much greater than a calf," I said. "He taught you a trade. And now he'd want you to use that trade to care for your mother."

His pace slowed, just for an instant, then resumed. I had found his weakness. "Come work for me," I said. "You'll oversee all my laborers, in every village. You'll never have to lift an adze again, and your mother will have whatever she needs until the end of her days."

He was tempted, I could tell. But then he stood, stiff-necked, to face me. "I must carry on my father's business," he said.

James, behind me, drew in his breath sharply. Anger filled my heart. I had come to this young carpenter in a spirit of kindness, with an offer most men would die for, and this was how he repaid me? I was accustomed to such arrogance from physicians and lawyers, but I'd be damned if I took it from a common grain of salt.

I smiled at him coldly. "Then I wish you success."

As I turned to leave, I noticed the little box among his wares and picked it up. Oak and square, it was the length of my hand and half as deep. And light as a dove but so sturdy that I could have used it as a hammer. The lid slid along grooves—a simple design, but I'd never seen it wrought so skillfully in a box this small. If I could produce it in bulk, I'd make a tenfold profit off each one, and he'd never sell another again. "I've taken much of your time," I said. "Let me buy this as a token of my thanks."

"If you like it, please take it." He spoke to me as if I were a child.

I opened my bag of silver and removed two coins. "Trust me, I can afford to pay."

"Thank you, but I have no need of your money."

I dropped the entire bag on the table. "Everyone needs money." The bag contained more silver than he could earn in a year, but he refused even to glance at it.

"I know this manner of man," I told James on our way back to Sepphoris. "He's already in his house, where no one else can see, counting the coins one by one."

And he'd know: That money came from me.

* * *

When I returned home, Martha was sitting on a bench in

the garden with a tunic in her lap, watching over the children. John dozed under a fig tree. Elizabeth marched a doll through an imaginary scene while Luke tossed pebbles in the air and counted how many he could catch. It was too peaceful to last. Sure enough, tiring of his game, Luke threw a pebble at the doll and knocked it over. Elizabeth punched him in the shoulder, and he whimpered.

If only Elizabeth were a boy. I couldn't imagine either son ever running my business.

Martha made room for me on the bench, and I sat next to her. She asked about my day, but before I could answer, Luke spotted the box in my hands and hurried over to inspect it. He had already forgotten about his shoulder.

"What do you think of it?" I asked.

He opened the lid, dropped his pebbles inside, and closed it up. The pebbles made a joyful noise when he shook the box, and he laughed. "Like a timbrel," he said. "Can I have it?"

Elizabeth grabbed the box out of his hands and dumped out the pebbles. Her doll fit inside it snugly. "This could be her bed!" she exclaimed. Even John roused himself and demanded to hold it.

Their reactions provoked me. I had built them this mansion with this beautiful garden, and the only thing that impressed them was a wooden box.

"It's lovely," Martha said. She, too, had fallen under its spell. "Did one of your workers make it?" She removed the doll and replaced it with a spool of thread that I hadn't noticed before. So that's why the tunic was on her lap; she'd been repairing it. I employed four maidservants, yet Martha did their work for them, as if she were married to a gardener.

I grabbed the spool from the box and held it in the air between us. "Don't we have servants?" I asked.

"I enjoy it. And what else would I do all day while you're traveling across Galilee?"

"I travel across Galilee so no one in my family will ever have to sew."

She made a sound between a laugh and a groan. "Right. I keep forgetting."

I was too vexed to argue with her. I took the box and went inside to a private room where I could be alone. Where had this carpenter gained such skill? Not from Joseph, verily. I slid the top of the box open and closed and open again, searching for its secret. I hadn't built anything with my own hands in many years. But even at my best, could I have matched it?

I pushed the question aside. I had chosen my path long ago, and I had no regrets. Anyone could be a carpenter, but I employed dozens of them. Tomorrow I would speak to James.

* * *

Three weeks went by. While I waited, I bought a vineyard near Tiberias. James found it for me. I was running out of ways to expand my construction business, and I already supplied other vineyards with barrels and presses. So it was a shrewd decision financially—not to mention something that no carpenter from Nazareth would ever accomplish.

Then it came to pass one morning that James placed four boxes on a table in the garden: the one from Joseph's son and, lined up in a row, three others of the same size. I put a few pebbles in the first one and shook it; the rattle was dull and somber, so I set it aside. The second box was too heavy; I didn't even open it.

The last was the most beautiful of the three. My hopes rose; this would be the one. But when I placed Elizabeth's doll inside, the box wouldn't close.

"These three were the best of them?" I asked.

"Yes," James said quietly.

All over Galilee, my carpenters were beginning their labors. They went wherever I commanded them to go and built whatever I commanded them to build. But not him. I felt like a shepherd with a hundred sheep until one wandered away. No matter where I searched or how loudly I called, it refused to come. The other ninety-nine meant nothing to me; all I wanted was the one I couldn't have.

Someone needed to suffer for this. If not Joseph's son, someone else. I swept the three boxes off the table.

James looked at me, his dark eyes full of sorrow. He leaned over to pick up the box closest to him, pinning it between his left arm and torso. When he tucked the second box next to it, both slipped through his grasp and dropped to the ground. Sighing, he gathered them and set them on the table. Then he retrieved the third one, returned it to the table, and stacked all three, topping them with his tablet. Lifting the stack from the bottom, he leaned it against his chest and secured it with his chin. His sandals scraped the ground as he slowly left my sight, afraid to lift his feet for fear of dropping the boxes all over again.

Alone now, I walked to the southern edge of the garden. Sepphoris lay below me. Wherever I looked, I saw my handiwork: houses, walls, gates, towers. I had built them to last for generations. And in the distance, beyond my vision, was Nazareth.

Everyone had a price. He was no different than anyone

else.

* * *

This time, I traveled without James. I wanted to have this conversation alone.

The old blind man was under the same tree, still banging his cup. His sandals seemed new, but perhaps I had overlooked them on my earlier visit. Either way, he didn't need my charity.

When I arrived at the shop, the carpenter was speaking to a small group of men gathered in a half circle around him. I stood a few cubits apart, close enough to listen.

"There was a certain man who owned a vineyard," he said.

I gasped. Was he speaking about me? How did he know I'd bought one? But he continued his story; he meant someone else, of course. This man, he said, hired some workers early in the morning and offered to pay each one a denarius. Later, he hired more workers, and in the afternoon, still more. When the sun set, all received the same wage: a denarius.

The man nearest me interrupted. He had broad shoulders with a sunburned neck and looked as if he'd labored in his share of vineyards. "That's not fair," he said. "Those who worked longer should get more pay."

"Let's ask our visitor," the carpenter said. "What do you think, Timothy?"

The others turned toward me, and I felt the weight of their stares. Suddenly I was back in Torah school, a young boy again, struggling to name the twelve tribes of Israel while my classmates laughed at me behind their hands. I shook off the memory and spoke with a confidence I didn't feel.

"Did the owner pay each man the amount he agreed to work for?"

"He did."

"Then the workers have no cause to complain."

He nodded at me and smiled. "Timothy is right," he said. "It's the owner's money. He can do with it what he will."

I felt a gladness in my heart that confounded me, and I chastised myself. Of course I had answered correctly. I didn't need this young carpenter's approval. When had he ever hired any workers? I was the only master here.

The others soon departed, leaving the two of us. Joseph's son turned his attention to a piece of limestone and prepared to cut it. I didn't know why he bothered; nothing would come of such a worthless stone.

"Have you reconsidered my offer?" I asked. He picked up a chisel but didn't answer. With no more customers around, his arrogance had returned. "You know I'm a wealthy man."

He smote the stone, and a piece fell to the ground. "Indeed," he said at last. "And my neighbors are grateful. Thanks to your silver, the hungry were fed, the homeless have shelter, the poor have new clothes."

A moment passed before I realized what he meant. "That money was for you," I said.

"Yes, but the owner can do whatever he wants with it, don't you agree?" He smiled as if pleased with himself. "You think I took the credit for helping those people? And then when they need a craftsman, they'll hire me instead of one of your workers?"

I wanted to deny it but could not. He chiseled off another piece of stone.

"I told them the money came from Timothy of Sepphoris, the builder."

Was he possessed by devils? What would it gain him to praise a rival? Then, in an instant, I understood. He knew he could never equal what I had achieved. As hard as he labored, and even with his great skill, he would never be more than a common carpenter. So he pretended that he had no need of worldly possessions, that he was happier poor and unknown than I would ever be with my wealth and fame. That's why he rejected my offer to provide for his mother. That's why he gave away my silver. He was trying to turn the tables on me. To make me covet his way of life. But I was on to him now.

* * *

The next morning, I explained my plan to James. I would send my two best laborers to Nazareth. If Joseph's son charged six denarii to build a wall, they should charge three. They could even work for free. I'd make up the difference in their wages. Whatever it took to drive him out of business and out of my life. James wrote down my instructions in silence. If he disagreed with me, he knew better than to say so. Not after failing me with the boxes.

My laborers were soon busy in Nazareth while Joseph's son worked less and less. Within a week, James reported, no one was hiring him at all.

"What does he do all day while my workers are taking his wages?" I pointed to James's tablet. "Read it to me."

"He tells stories," James said. "People gather at his shop to listen." He read from his notes. "One was about a buried treasure. A certain man found it in a field, but he didn't want anyone to know about it. So he saved up all his money and—"

I cut him off. First vineyards, now buried treasures. I had no patience for stories. "Does he try to sell them anything? Has he made any more boxes?"

"No," James said, "the people just asked him questions and he answered them. Or sometimes he asked them questions."

"He's up to something," I said. "Find out what it is."

The next morning, James reported that the crowd had grown. Entire families attended, even little children. "He stood on a table so everyone could hear him. He talked about a king who held a wedding banquet for his son and invited—"

I held up my hand. "Again, he did no work?"

"None."

"Does he ask anyone for money? Or food?"

James shook his head.

It made no sense. How long could he last without wages? Telling stories wouldn't feed his mother.

"If you wish," James said, "I could return to his workshop today and see."

He was facing the sun, so his eyes were narrowed and wrinkled at the corners. His tightly curled hair had turned gray, but he was still James the Lesser, still my faithful disciple. I wondered how long he would have waited until I answered. An hour? All morning? My heart was moved; I shouldn't have made him pick up those boxes.

"Yes," I said. "Go."

* * *

But, lo, James didn't return the next morning. This had never happened before. He was in good health and knew I was expecting a report. Was his head so filled with buried treasures and wedding banquets that he'd forgotten who he worked for?

Hours passed. I tried to occupy myself with other matters. My vineyard was producing only half the yield that I'd been promised, and I should have summoned the steward to provide an account. But I couldn't stop thinking about Joseph's son. Why was he gathering customers to his shop if not to sell them goods? Did he have some other source of income? Then I remembered my bag of silver, and suddenly I understood. He hadn't given it all away—he'd only pretended to do so while hoarding the largest portion for himself. He was a hypocrite, no better than the priests at the synagogue! And oh, how he must be laughing at me, living like a king with my money.

I put on my cloak and set out to confront him face-to-face. I walked quickly, my anger burning hotter with each step. I would hear no more of his stories, no more clever words that troubled my heart. He would return my silver and depart from Galilee at once, or I would beat him until his dying breath.

But when I arrived at his shop, no one was there. The table was empty, and the tools had vanished.

An elderly man walked by, muttering to himself as if possessed. I called to him. "The carpenter—have you seen him?"

The man began laughing for no reason and pointing here and there. "I see the house, I see the tree, I see the sky, I see—"

I grabbed him roughly by the shoulders. "Joseph's son. Where is he?"

"I don't know." He was still laughing. "I saw him yesterday, but I don't see him today."

I shoved him aside, and the old man staggered away. Had I won? I wanted the carpenter of Nazareth to leave, and, lo, he had departed. But where was he now? Perhaps he had moved to another village to open a new shop. Yes, that must be it. He said he wanted to continue his father's business—he must have fled somewhere he thought he could escape me. If so, he was mistaken. Did he not know how far my reach extended? All my workers, in every village, would watch for him. Wherever the sheep wandered, I would track him down.

And if he continued to defy me? What would I do then? My thoughts turned violent as I pondered the price he would pay.

I wished then that I could speak with James. He had observed the carpenter many times; perhaps he could discern where he was hiding. Again, I wondered why he didn't come to my garden this morning. Could he have already begun the hunt? Of course! That was the only possible explanation. As soon as he'd discovered the carpenter was missing, he must have set out to look for him. He might be with him at this very moment.

Good man, James. No one was more loyal. A friend, even. I would discuss the matter with him tomorrow. He would surely return tomorrow.

* * *

This story first appeared in the After Dinner Conversation—April 2023 issue.

Discussion Questions

1. Timothy the builder has a specific perspective and life focus. How would you describe it? Is he unique or wrong to have that perspective and life focus? What are the benefits and detriments of his life focus?

2. On several occasions, Timothy the builder incorrectly interprets the motivations of Joseph's son. Why is Timothy unable to understand the young carpenter's motivations?

3. What characteristic allows certain individuals to be better (*or worse*) at perspective shifting?

4. What could Timothy the builder have done to better understand and believe the motivations of Joseph's son rather than continuing to see them through his own perspective?

5. Is it wrong to simply want to work, become successful, and take care of your family as Timothy has done? Why is Timothy an unsympathetic character in this story?

* * *

Guilt-Edge Security

James A. Hartley

* * *

I sat beside the bar rubbing my glass across polished mahogany and watching trails of moisture it left behind. It must have cost them a fortune to ship real wood way out to the Rim. It didn't look synthetic. I looked over at the barman and he tossed his head, then went back to polishing the glasses. Real authentic stuff. I was nursing my fourth bourbon when the guy walked in.

He was a florid, heavy-set guy and I could just tell he was a salesman. He had the suit, he had the haircut, and he had the little case. Maybe things would have been different if it had been a different night.

He swaggered up to the bar and planted himself like he owned the place. Maybe he did. He raised two fingers and the barman filled a glass with what looked like scotch. He drained the first one quickly, then signaled for another. When his second arrived, he turned to scan the bar. I studied him out of the corner of my eye. Finally, he turned and looked at me, nodded then smiled. Another quick circuit of the room and he slid his drink down the bar toward me.

"Hey, Mac," he said to me. "Mind if I join you?"

I shrugged and motioned to the place beside me. Looking back, that might have been the big mistake.

"You're in the game, right?" he said. "You look like the sort. Marketing and sales, right? No other reason for being out in this backwater. Let me guess. You're from Earth." I nodded and he grinned.

"Yeah, me too. Jack. Jack Davis's the name." He thrust a meaty paw toward me, and I shook it.

"Steve Walker," I said.

"So, what are you drinking, Steve," he said. I pointed at my bourbon and he motioned to the barman and pointed to both our glasses. I didn't mind. If this Jack Davis was going to buy me drinks, I could put up with a pitch. I guessed that was what was coming. If I listened, he'd probably buy me drinks all night. I wouldn't have to sign anything, and I'd walk away at the end several bourbons better off.

"Well, Steve, it's lucky I ran across you. You and me being in the same game, you'll understand what I'm talking about. Let me ask you a question, Steve. What do you think about integrity?"

It was a funny sort of question.

"How do you mean?"

"Well, you know, you and me both, we're in sales. Is integrity a part of that?"

"I still don't..."

"Okay, maybe I need to make it a bit clearer. You ever hear of a place called Galipienzo?" I pressed my lips together and shook my head. He nodded. "Yeah, well, neither had I. Then I sort of bumped into the place. You know how it is."

I nodded my head to humor him and glanced significantly at my glass. He grinned and waved the barman over.

"The way I got involved was pretty simple," he said. "I'd been doing the Rim, selling a line of high-tech components to the emerging markets. Some of those Rim worlds had a lot of promise at the time. The returns were meager, but you have to have vision in this game. Am I right?" I nodded and looked attentive. The bourbon was good.

"You sell them a bit of tech, they build on that, then they start wanting bigger and better things. It was a good market, or, at least, it had potential to be.

"I was just on the verge of getting somewhere with my collection of Rim worlds, when I ran into Galipienzo. I got too greedy I suppose. Wanted to add one more sleeper to the list. I didn't know too much about the place at the time. It had all the right criteria, out on the Rim, fairly isolated, not in the commercial mainstream. I thought it would be easy. Maybe if I'd gotten there about two centuries earlier. Oh, I did business there, good business, but in a place like Galipienzo, good business takes time."

I was starting to wonder if this was a pitch after all. The things Davis was saying made sense. I knew what it was like out there at the hard edge on the Rim.

"The thing about doing business in a society like that is, you've got to be able to work the hierarchies. That takes patience. I had to grease the right palms, get to know the connections and the faces. That led me to other names and faces. Gradually my network started to grow. Word of mouth is the best sales tool you can get, right?"

"Yeah, don't I know it," I said. "That's why we're out here pounding the beat, winning their confidence."

"Right, Steve," said Davis. "Well, the Galipienzans were a cautious lot — always looking for the sting. That drew the process out. I was there maybe two, three months in all. Long enough to work out how the place worked, long enough to know that the only way I was going to do real business was with the Lord himself. Now, that's only a title, Steve. He's not a deity or anything, though he might as well have been. Sheesh, if you could've seen the guy..."

I smiled. I'd known a few like that in my time.

"Anyway, one of the first things I learned about the Galipienzans was that they liked to *own* things. It didn't matter what, but property was status. One way to own things was to dispossess your fellow natives. If they ran out of fellow Galipienzans, they looked elsewhere. Most of the other worlds didn't like them very much. I didn't like them very much — arrogant, sneering opinionated bastards, and that's their good side. It meant they weren't very good at doing business. They couldn't market themselves, you see. That's where I came in to the picture.

"Kayzoro, the Lord, had a product, but he didn't have anyone to market it for him. He knew he couldn't rely on his fellow Galipienzans to go out and have any chance of success. The only way he was going to achieve the status he desired was to own as much as he could of the known worlds. The only way to do that was to take out rights on the basic integrity of a few key individuals — possession by proxy."

Suddenly, I was confused again. I had no idea what he was talking about, but the man was buying my drinks, so I persisted.

"What do you mean by rights on integrity, Jack? I don't see how that factors in."

Davis sipped at his scotch and put down his glass. He ran his fingers through the beaded moisture on its side, then turned and fixed me with a serious expression.

"Listen, Steve," he said after a pause. "You have every right to ask that question. What place is there for integrity... say call it a person's soul... in the hard-nosed reality of these days of FTL travel? It's true, the known universe is no longer what it used to be, and we don't believe in the sort of stuff we used to. Occasionally I tell people to take the time to browse for a definition of 'soul'. 'Don't let me stop you,' I tell them. I'm sure you'll find the answers. The accumulated knowledge of generations is at your fingertips."

"Yeah, and..."

"I guess what I'm saying is that I believe in integrity. In other words, I believe in souls, but maybe not in the way others think about them. It's a question of morality. For me, the soul is about having the ability to choose, to make your own decisions based upon your own understanding of what's right and wrong. Take away that right from someone, that freedom to choose, and you own his or her *soul* or whatever you want to call it. It took me a long time to understand that. By the time I realized that, it was too late — too late for me and too late for a lot of others."

I was starting to think I'd run into a religious nut and any moment he was going to come out with the pamphlets. But I was interested now, and the muzzy bourbon effect was softening my tolerance.

"Okay, Steve," he said. "Look around. Look at all the worlds out there. Sure, these worlds have elective processes, but behind all that, there's always someone who ultimately pulls the strings. You think these guys have souls, free will? They might have had once. Have you noticed how most of the big industrialists and people like that seem to have been around for a long, long time? The only way they've managed to do that is to lose part of themselves. I know how. I know exactly how they've managed to do it. They've given up the freedom to choose. Someone else calls the shots for them. Now, in my book, if they don't have that freedom, they've lost what we could loosely call their *soul*."

"So, what are you telling me, Jack?" I asked. "Is this some sort of religious spiel? You going to save my soul?"

"No, no. Sorry, Steve," he said. "Here, let me get you another drink." He motioned for the barman. "I'm getting a little ahead of myself."

The barman filled our glasses, and Davis stared down at them, then nodded and waited for the barman's retreat before continuing. He traced a pattern on the bar surface, pursed his lips, and then turned.

"Let me fill you in on Galipienzo. It might start to make more sense."

I took another sip at my bourbon — my sixth, or seventh. I'd lost count.

"Galipienzo started small, but as a world it had all the ingredients to make it something great. It sat isolated on the Rim for decades, a backwater overlooked by the trading communities and mainstream commerce around it. The world could have smoldered and sparked then flared back into non-existence, ignored by the rest of humanity, but Galipienzo had something special. You see they had their own little scientific community. It interacted with the rest of the research community, but somehow they were on their own."

I'd seen worlds like that myself, but I still didn't see where this was going.

"What Galipienzo had to keep them apart was unique. The world was home to a tiny molecular structure." Davis held up his thumb and forefinger and peered through the gap between them. "That structure became known to the Galipienzan research community and the beauty of it was that it defied analysis unless you knew how. That was their great discovery — how to analyze the stuff. They weren't going to tell anyone else how to do it.

"They worked out they had a good thing going as soon as they found out how to apply their little compound. As far as anyone can work out, it's the only means of producing the gene repressor that controls longevity. Think about it. I mean really think about it. Do you understand the implications?"

I nodded and licked my lips.

"So, what did they do? They bottled the stuff of course. Called it *Life*. A great name, don't you think? Beautiful marketing strategy. I wish I'd thought of it."

"So, if they've got this stuff, why haven't I seen it?" I asked him. "I would've thought it'd be all over the marketplace."

"You would have thought so, wouldn't you? But it didn't work like that. They had this stuff for, say about three hundred years, before it hit the broader byways. Think about it. You have an isolated community and suddenly it has access to this stuff that prolongs life span by a factor of three, four or five. What happens? First, the population expands at an amazing rate. More people, longer life span, natural selection steps in. What's a life here or there along the way? People became disposable resources. Hell of an environment to grow up in.

"For a couple of hundred years that worked admirably. They got on with their business and we got on with ours. That was until Kayzoro clawed his way to the top of the heap. Finally, the Galipienzans had someone in charge who wasn't satisfied with his own little piece of real estate. The problem was, this guy was not just your run-of-the-mill expansionist head case. He was smart. He had that unusual combination of brains and strength.

"I told you how they like to own things. Kayzoro knew Galipienzo had its limitations. What was it — some small hick planet out in the sticks? He knew that if some tin-pot nation suddenly started going military, he'd have all of the combined forces of the known worlds down on him in less time than you could say 'response force'. Whatever else, you have to admire him for his smarts."

Davis leaned back and sighed. "Personally, I can't stand him. Nasty piece of work...Anyway, where was I? Oh yes, he had a far better way of conquering civilization. He had the ready-made tool at his fingertips. He had *Life*."

The bells of opportunity were ringing faintly in the back of my head, even through the bourbon haze.

"So, what's your involvement?" I asked.

Davis shrugged. "I'd been working the Galipienzan market for some time and finally I managed to work my way up to Kayzoro himself. Oh, he wanted some of what I had to sell, no trouble there. It was just how he paid me. If only I'd had the foresight to see what was going on then. He knew exactly what he was doing. After that, *I* didn't have any choice. What would you have done in my position? There I was and he was offering me the chance of a lifetime — literally. He paid me for my first consignment in *Life*. By the time we got to the third, I was hooked. It was then that he made me an offer, and how could I refuse? There it was, guaranteed income and my own personal supply direct from the source."

He took a deep swallow from his drink. "He used me to hook a few of the others in over time. We're all in the same game after all. We talk, compare notes, swap war stories. It was easy enough to do. I guess, in a way, we do business despite rather than because of him. We act as our own little support network. Regardless, you've got to have faith in the product to do good business. That's how it works. And I've certainly got faith in the product. As for job security, there's nothing to beat it."

"So why didn't you tell him to stuff his product? Why didn't you just demand payment?"

He looked at me for a long time before answering.

"When you get to a certain age, your mortality begins to tell. You've felt it, Steve. You start to slow down, feel the strain, become less enthusiastic. You start to think about how long you've got left and what you have left to do. How can you seriously pass up an opportunity like that? You can't. You'd sell your own soul for the chance to escape that terminus — anyone would. And that applies just as much to your leading industrialists and power brokers across the known worlds. You see why I was talking about souls before? Kayzoro knew that, and he knew the power it could give him. Just imagine the prospect of having the means to deny death within the palm of your hand. What would you give to have that power? He knew he had me."

I nodded slowly.

Davis continued looking at me intently.

"Remember how I asked you about integrity?"

"Uh-huh."

"Well, the truth of it is, I never had any intention of compromising my integrity, you have to understand that. When it came to it, I didn't have much choice. Doing business across the multiple worlds can be a hell of a task at the best of times, but with Kayzoro calling the shots it was really difficult. Integrity just didn't come into it. I suppose I could have had a choice, but he owned me by then. What could I do?"

Davis retrieved his case from the floor, flipped it open and reached inside.

"Look at me," he said, without looking at me. "How old do you think I am? Forty? Fifty? Well I'll tell you. Two hundred and six next birthday."

I almost dropped my glass.

Davis smiled and nodded slowly. "Anyway, I've been talking to you for too long." He reached into the case and pulled something out. "Here, let me leave you with this. It's just a sampler of our new product line. We call it *Rejuve*. Cute little bottle. See the way it glows? That one's yours to keep."

"Um, thanks," I said, looking down at the small glass tube lying in my hand.

Davis got to his feet. "Well, it's been good to meet you, Steve. I'll see you next time I'm through this way — in about eight years. We'll talk some more then. You'll be here."

He nodded to the barman and walked out.

That was eight years ago to the day. Now I'm sitting in that same bar. Maybe if I'd realized what a good pitch it was, things would have been different. But I didn't, and I'm sitting watching the door, hoping that he'll show. There's a half-full glass of bourbon on the bar beside me, and a small, empty bottle in my hand.

* * *

This story first appeared in the After Dinner Conversation—May 2021 issue.

Discussion Questions

1. If you were in the narrator's position, would you drink the bottle of *Rejuve* that was handed to you?
2. Assuming you did drink the bottle of *Rejuve* and it did work as advertised, would you be back for more of it eight years later?
3. What would change about the way you live your life, if you knew you were going to live 400 or 500 years?
4. Does the threat of impending death affect how you live your life? In what way? Does knowing you have a limited amount of time make each day, and each choice, more precious? Would a nearly unlimited life span spoil that preciousness and urgency?
5. Kayzoro believed that if too many people knew they had discovered *Life* they would be invaded for their resource, do you agree? How is this pattern similar, or different, compared to when a country on earth discovers it has an abundance of a limited resource, like oil or diamonds?

* * *

The Money Box

Phillip Scott Mandel

* * *

This is not a morality tale. It's simply a story.

It began innocently enough, over a lunch of beef pho in the Financial District, when my friend Paolo first mentioned the Money Box. Paolo was a pupa of industry then, waiting to emerge as a titan. He was wearing a light blue seersucker suit with a flower-print ascot, which I remember distinctly because he spilled Sriracha on it. Also it was unseasonably cold for May, yet Paolo made us take a table outside.

"A money box?" I said, intrigued.

He nodded, dabbing at his lapel with a wet napkin. "I can show you one day."

"What's with the getup, anyway?" I said. "Are you going to the Derby?"

"Oh, I've no need of such action anymore," he replied, smiling cryptically. He slurped a noodle through a straw-shaped gap in his lips and changed the subject to his upcoming wedding, to which I was invited, though with no honorifics.

Paolo, unfortunately, I have not seen in ages. Swept up like the rest of us, I suppose, in the season of the plague.

* * *

Months passed with no mention of the Money Box, and I tried to forget about it. The news was awash with rising sea levels and apocalyptic dust storms. That summer was, yet again, the hottest on record. One of my clients suffered an oil refinery explosion that destroyed four hundred thousand acres of virgin rainforest. Another client published a series of tweets denying the Holocaust. So I had plenty to think about. But I couldn't stop obsessing over the Money Box.

I threw myself in with my colleagues, whom I despised, and I walked my dog, whom I loved. I tried to date, with little success. My ears are rubbery and pinguid, my mouth spumescent. My nostrils are asymmetrical and, as an object, my body is short and round, unpleasing to the eye. A small but noticeable goiter protrudes from my neck. Also, I don't ever seem to "get" jokes and therefore must force myself to laugh, often inappropriately.

Nevertheless, I was able to charm one woman, Penelope, in for a nightcap. It was our eleventh date, and her children were with her sister. When I flipped on the lights I noticed my goldfish, Simeon, had finally succumbed to the dropsy. He had indeed looked singularly unhappy for weeks, swimming in circles and popping out little air bubbles, but in my malaise I'd done nothing about it. So she wouldn't see Simeon's inert body floating at the top of the bowl, I had Penelope wait in the kitchen while I scooped him out with a little net and deposited his rotted carcass into the toilet. He seemed to be staring up at me with those piteous, lifeless eyes, forever open and plaintive, as (regretfully, I admit) I urinated on him, for I didn't want to waste a flush.

* * *

I didn't tell Penelope about the Money Box, nor did I pester Paolo about it.

But many nights I would dream fitfully about it, though I knew nothing other than it was *called* a "Money Box." My imagination cooked up all manner of containers: an old cigarette carton stuffed with hundreds; a gleaming, stainless steel bank vault stacked with bricks of gold bullion; or more banally, a bulging chest of diamonds, rubies, and other treasure, protected by a scaly, halitotic dragon.

I was distracted, and perhaps because of this, four Key Accounts under my purview—including the ruinously careless energy company, and the anti-Semite—left our firm in Q3. My manager Rick (I've never trusted anyone named Rick) had HR write me up. Maybe he just couldn't stand the look of me any longer. I can't say I blame him.

Was I fired? No. Too much paperwork, Rick explained. But I might polish a CV. He'd provide a lukewarm reference.

"I am not a feudal serf!" I screamed, right in his face, then slammed his office door.

Of course but I did neither of those things. Because we both knew I *was*, in fact, a serf, quite dutifully bound to that hateful square of carpet upon which rested my cubicle, and my personhood was owned, if not by Rick, then by our shareholders.

Even Penelope broke off our budding romance, saying I always seemed distracted, never "present," as if I was seeing someone else.

Even then, I failed to mention the Money Box.

"Look at me, Penny," I said. "Do you think I'm seeing someone else?"

She shook her head sadly and said, "That doesn't make me feel any better."

* * *

Finally Paolo invited me to his house for a dinner party. His fiancée, Erin, was there, as were six other corporatized schlogs, so I brought my dachshund, Tyrone. Everybody loves a dachshund, and the guests of this dinner party proved no exception.

Erin was the kind of woman who decorated her home—a narrow, red-brick townhouse amid a row of old townhouses— with electric tea lights instead of real ones, who posted photos of her meals, a person who could never allow natural lulls in conversation to stand. While I was chewing on a particularly fatty piece of brisket and therefore could not stop her, she detailed her and Paolo's honeymoon itinerary, about which I had not inquired. Then she rolled her eyes and said, "I've already been there," as if I might sympathize with her dilemma. "Eight years ago." She scanned the room and lowered her voice. "With my ex."

I bowed, unsure what else to do. I'd heard from Paolo that Steve (her ex) was a loathsome brute, but had, for some reason, managed to remain friends with Erin and was even invited to the wedding.

"It's a remarkable place," she continued. "Really. The people are so warm, so friendly. Always smiling. But the flies, my god. Bigger than bumblebees. Their wings sound like static on the radio."

I didn't have the heart to tell her that the place had been flooded into near extinction and these "friendly people" were now refugees, and had, if they were lucky, absconded to more moderate climes, or at least higher ground.

After dessert, Paolo brought out the Money Box. "I know this is why you're here," he said, over half-hearted protests that we'd come for his company. "This is what you came to see."

In the corner of the room, there were two rolled-up foam mats—the yellow one more frayed than its purple cousin—peeking out from under a white bar cart, and I was momentarily struck with a bolt of intense sorrow, a hollow pain in my gut, both for my own loneliness and for imagining this soon-to-be-married couple doing yoga together.

Presently Erin cleared the plates and silverware and empty crystal punch bowl centerpiece, and Paolo placed the Money Box on the table.

It was jet black and perfectly cubical: roughly 18 inches per side, the size of a small guitar amp, or a cheap ottoman from Ikea. I don't know if it was painted, or what onyx material the box was made of, but no light reflected off its surface. It emitted no smell or sound, and I imagined if I'd touched my tongue to it, I would taste nothing. But I did seem to feel a slight warmth emanated from where it sat on the table, just out of arm's reach.

Despite my intense curiosity, the Money Box was, in a way, terror-inducing. What astronauts must feel on their first spacewalk, staring into that infinite midnight, or the day after someone wins the lottery.

On all six sides of the cube was a slit in the center. I didn't notice until Paolo pointed them out, and then I couldn't take my eyes away. The ever-slightest glow seeped from each aperture, as if the box was filled with a weak incandescent bulb.

"It doesn't matter what side you lay the Money Box on," Paolo said. "It all works the same way."

"But what does it do?" Steve said.

"Just wait," Paolo said, as if expecting the interruption. "Someone give me some money."

Steve gave Paolo a dollar bill. I suddenly found I didn't care for Steve, and not only out of loyalty to Paolo, but because earlier in the night he'd been pontificating about Robert Rauschenberg.

"No, something higher."

Dee-Ann, with her suede jacket and designer purse, handed him a luminous gold credit card with an ovate portrait of a centurion in the center, buying her a few chuckles 'round the table.

"That'll work," Paolo said, but as he went to take it from her, she pulled back her arm with an almost imperceptible hiccup. Dee-Ann, always so composed, was coming undone by this frightening device. We all were.

Finally, Sanjeev took a crisp hundred-dollar bill out of his billfold. He ran one of the sharpest hedge funds in the world.

"Perfect," Paolo said, and grabbed it.

"Wait," Sanjeev said, but by then Paolo had already inserted it into the Money Box.

It happened so quickly I barely registered the transaction. The bill went into the slit smoothly, like buying a Coke at a vending machine, and then... Nothing.

We stared at each other. There was no sound, no movement, just our eyes darting back and forth, skeptically, between the box and ourselves.

Tyrone barked. "Hush," I said, and bent down to scratch his ear.

That's why I missed what happened when these people—my non-friend acquaintances—gasped and said, collectively, "Oh."

I popped back up to see Sanjeev holding three fifty-dollar bills, and Paolo holding a finsky.

Sanjeev cleared his throat. "How the hell—"

"It's the Money Box," Paolo said, with a grim smile, like a dentist extracting a persnickety, stuck tooth. "Who else wants a turn?"

* * *

Perhaps I should take a moment to provide context for what happened next.

The Assyrians of Nineveh worshipped a minor deity, the Locust Man, as God of Agriculture (maternal uncle to the Goddess of Fertility). The Scythians called this same divine spirit the Patron of Slavery, and in the earliest known version of the Hebrew Bible, he is alternately referred to as "Trust-King" and the "Grandfather of Suffering." Ancient Hindus referred to him as the ex-boyfriend of Lakshmi.

Unsurprisingly, only human sacrifice would do for such a god.

A few tiny sects of contemporary monotheistic religions still claim him as the precursor to Jehovah, but he is not. His true identity is the Lord of Money and Pestilence. That is all.

There is a well-guarded and little-known archive of religious artifacts in the sub-sub-basement of the Peace Palace in The Hague wherein lies an ivory carving—a woolly mammoth tusk, in fact, not unlike the Lion-man of

Hohlenstein-Stadel—of a humanoid figure with a finely detailed orthopterous head, leathery forewings and membranous hind wings, and two razor-sharp chewing mandibles. It's as close a simulacrum to the Locust Man's true form as you'll find in the modern world.

I know all this because, since the plague season commenced, I've done a whole lot of research on the subject.

* * *

Anyway, nobody knew how the Money Box worked. I hesitate, even, to say "worked," because the box didn't appear to *do* anything.

It was easy to demonstrate *that* it worked: I saw with my own eyes people insert countless hundred-dollar bills and receive back larger sums of money, though always in smaller denominations—and Paolo always got his cut. But the box itself made no noise, and there appeared to be no machinery inside, no moving parts. At first, we guessed there was a wireless or Bluetooth device: a money-counter, or a copy machine, printing out fake currency.

But the Money Box produced authentic legal tender, indeed. I bought clothes and lottery tickets and Uber Eats and deposited it in my account with no trouble.

Whenever the box was "processing," as it were, nobody could sense any type of disturbance. But Tyrone would whimper. That, I suppose, should have been a tip-off something beyond merely cryptic, but untoward, and unnatural, was taking place, though I couldn't ascertain what. But there are a lot of things in the physical world that exist, that are real, but are also mysterious and imperceptible, like quantum entanglement, gamma radiation, germs, evolution, or falling in and out of love.

I don't disbelieve such phenomena just because I can't perceive, or make sense of, them with my lowly consciousness and imperfect naked eye.

Paolo would not say where he got the Money Box, and he certainly wouldn't take it out of his home. If you wanted to use it, you had to be invited. And you had to bring cash. There appeared to be no limit to the amount of money the thing would convert—as long as you used increments of fifty-dollar bills or higher. And you could recycle the same bills: if you put in a hundred, and got back three fifties, you could put one of those fifties back in and get three twenties (Paolo would get a single dollar from such a meager exchange). Indeed, Dee-Ann came back from London with a £50 note and got back four twenties, which was even better than the currency exchange rate (incidentally, she also put in €100 and received a less generous exchange). However, if you put in a twenty or smaller, the money simply disappeared.

I was invited to Paolo's house three more times before the wedding, and on my second visit, I brought ten fresh one-hundred-dollar bills. He'd bought a case of Veuve Clicquot and it was a crowded, celebratory, almost raucous dining table.

But, even tipsy as I was, it was then I noticed Paolo himself never used the Money Box, and I began to grow suspicious. I tried to ask him why, but he'd always dodge the question, or say something about "not getting high on your own supply."

Nevertheless, the third time I visited, I brought a wad of one-hundred-dollar bills (the extent of my life savings) and for a time after that, I felt, mistakenly, that I was a rich man.

This belief—and the ease with which I adopted the churlish smugness and imperious vanity that led me to tell off

Rick—was, perhaps, my tragic flaw. But he'd made me take down my inspirational poster of a wet grizzly bear eating a salmon, underneath which was the phrase, "Only when the last tree has been felled, the last river poisoned, and the last fish caught, will we remember that money cannot be eaten." He said it was antithetical to our company's mission and the passive voice was weak writing. So I told him where to stick it.

How could I have known?

In any case, on that third visit, Dee-Ann was present again. She was haughty as ever, complaining that Singapore Airlines was "going to seed."

"You shouldn't be flying at all," I muttered under my breath.

"Come again?" Sanjeev said, staring at me with disgust.

"Carbon emissions," Dee-Ann replied, rolling her eyes and smiling a vulgar little smile.

We were in Paolo's living room now, which had more room for guests. Every book Paolo owned was about predatory subprime mortgage lending, credit default swaps, Lehman Brothers. Old news.

Dee-Ann brought out that same glinting golden credit card from before. She handed it over to Paolo, confidently now, and, oddly, it appeared the centurion, in his oval, had reversed, now facing the left.

"You're sure?" Paolo said. Dee-Ann nodded.

Paolo inserted the credit card into the Money Box, and we waited. And waited.

"So anyone have weekend plans?" Erin said, in a newsprint-soft voice.

"Be quiet, please," Paolo said. I began to fret about how

long their marriage would last.

I'd booked Tyrone in a pet hotel for the night, but now I wished he was with me, if only to break the interminable silence with his jagged little yaps.

"What have you done?" Dee-Ann said eventually, alarmed.

"Just wait."

I concentrated, listening hard for any sound, such as the movement of infinitesimal gears or the laser scanning of a bar code. But nothing. It was like a séance.

"What the hell, Paolo?" Dee-Ann said. "Now I'm going to have to cancel it."

Paolo's eyes widened. "Do *not* do that. Whatever you do."

"Why not?"

We all stared at Paolo, and I felt a sensation of dread creep up from the pit of my stomach into my throat. It felt exactly like when, in business school, I'd downloaded an essay for an economics course and handed it in without even reading the damn thing. For weeks I waited to be expelled for plagiarism, but instead I received an A+.

Before Paolo could answer, the Money Box began spitting out hundred-dollar bills from all five slots. It was the hardest labor I'd seen from the machine. Ninety bills came out of each slot, for a total of forty-five thousand dollars. Paolo lifted the box, and there was another nine grand squished up under the bottom slot.

"Okay everyone," he said. "Time to go home."

"Wait," Dee-Ann said. "Where's my credit card?"

"It's gone."

"Gone where?"

Paolo and Erin started ushering people out of their house. "Just, gone," he said.

* * *

That was the first night I was visited by Mr. Locust. He was an evil, slender figure in a three-piece gray suit and he smelled like gasoline. He looked like a giant silverfish. In the dream I was tied to a hospital gurney, and under my body the icy metal bars burned my skin, for I was naked except for a pair of soiled white briefs. I couldn't understand what Mr. Locust was saying, but when he opened his mouth sometimes a dusty cricket would fly out. Suddenly he was holding a meat cleaver, like he intended to chop off my feet.

Despite my screams and protests, he removed everything below the ankle. It was not a quick process.

When he was done, I woke up. The lower half of my bed sheet was covered in blood, and my toenails were cracked and split apart, but my feet were still there, relatively intact.

I believe Paolo, in a benign yet insidious way (that is, without malice but without grace, either) sought to exploit the asymmetry of information between the market maker and the buyer, while skimming a little off the top for himself. A standard practice throughout human civilization—the oil in the gears of progress, in fact. The foundations of civilization. But did he *really* know how the Money Box worked? I don't think he did.

Not that it matters.

Steve was the first to be rejected by the Money Box. It turned out Steve was broke, though he claimed his money was tied up in "business ventures." We all knew it was booze, gambling, cocaine. Though I detested his personality, I didn't fault him his vices; as far as I was concerned, every man was free to swing his fist up to the tip of another man's nose, so to speak. But Steve, well, he was just rotten.

After that first rejection, Steve borrowed five hundred dollars—from whom I know not—and returned to Paolo's home, asking to use the Money Box to turn it into a thousand. Paolo refused. He said the money had to be earned.

Steve slapped him.

That's what Paolo told me. And why would Paolo lie? It's a humiliating thing, to be slapped by another man. To be infantilized, emasculated. After the slap, Paolo relented and let him use the Money Box, and Steve even kept Paolo's share.

As we neared the wedding, Paolo complained about Steve showing up at his house, clutching crinkled bills and asking for the Money Box, using words he obviously didn't understand, like "LIBOR" and "derivatives." Paolo said he wasn't an ATM, and eventually got a restraining order, but nobody believed Steve would be deterred by such weak tea. I think Steve planned to steal the Money Box, which would have been a disaster, as all economists and philosophers agree such power needs to be concentrated in few, competent hands; otherwise, society would devolve into an egalitarian, democratic wasteland. The unwashed masses are too ignorant to control their own urges, let alone steer the ship of culture. It would lead to anarchy, chaos, ruination.

Even the ancients knew as much.

Several opportunities passed for me to bring up Mr. Locust, who'd begun appearing in my dreams every second or third night. Paolo mentioned I looked like I wasn't getting enough sleep, and I was about to say something but even then, I held my tongue. Mr. Locust wasn't his problem, I told myself, though, really, I didn't want to make Mr. Locust angry. The phantom pain from his bullwhip and scalpel and wheel felt real enough, and there was no telling how Mr. Locust would punish me if I transgressed against him.

At first Penelope politely declined the invite to be my wedding date. I realized I'd grown quite fond of her, though, not unlike how, perhaps, a farmer grows fond of his favorite sow, or a gambler begins to trust his bookie. I enjoyed knowing her in the biblical sense, too, and after much prodding and begging, I convinced her to come.

"No funny stuff," she told me.

"I'm never funny," I replied, and relayed the old joke about the zombie and the chicken to prove it.

For Paolo's bachelor party, we scheduled a limousine to take us to a steakhouse, a casino, and a Gentlemen's Club. Before we left, I attempted to withdraw an enormous sum of cash from an ATM in preparation and was informed on the screen there was a problem with my account. This being a Saturday night, I figured I could handle it the following Monday.

Steve was not present, as he'd been disinvited.

Perhaps unsurprisingly, the steakhouse was in a sorry state of disrepair: a worn, frayed red rug led up a balustrade staircase missing several spindles into a nearly-empty dining room staffed by a crew of forlorn, phlegmatic waiters, all old enough to be waiting to die. It made me sad because it reminded me of my own father, who waited tables until the day he aneurismed in the walk-in fridge.

Before even the chateaubriand was served, Paolo's phone rang.

Steve had broken into their apartment, Erin said, and ransacked the place looking for the Money Box, all while brandishing a butterfly knife at her.

I could hear her tinny voice crying on the other side of the phone.

"That fool," Paolo breathed, shaking his head.

The bachelor party was cut short and the driver booked it on the highway back. 90 miles an hour is very fast for a limousine, and it felt like I was flying on a hovercraft.

When we got back Paolo told us to go home, not wanting anyone by his side when he called the authorities. Plausible deniability, he said.

"Paolo," I whispered, for I had a feeling I would never see him again.

"What?" He looked annoyed I hadn't left with the other guys.

"I wanted to ask—have you—in dreams—"

"You're asking me about the Man From Prehistory?"

"What?"

He shook his head and gently placed his hand on my arm. "I have to take care of this," he said. "Let's have brunch tomorrow. There is a ledger, you see. A grand, sort of mystical, ledger—it's hard to explain. You know how when a society cuts down all the trees, it collapses?"

I nodded, dumbfounded.

"Well, at some point, they had to decide to cut down that last tree, right?"

"Are we still talking about the Money Box?" I asked.

"Brunch, tomorrow," he said, ushering me away. "I'll fill you in on what I know."

Before I could respond, I found myself standing on the stoop, their front door locked and the window shades drawn. I ordered a car and waited near the street. My feet were tired and bruised from breaking in the stiff, polished patent leather oxfords I'd bought for the wedding.

A few minutes later my car showed up, and the driver was, to no surprise, Mr. Locust. Having no choice in the matter, I reluctantly but calmly got in the backseat. To my relief he did not engage in conversation on the ride home, other than to tell me how my father actually died.

Later I read in my medical file that the EMT from the ambulance told the triage nurse in the ER I'd lost so much blood he was sure I was a "goner."

* * *

I never saw Paolo again, or Steve, or the Money Box. The strips of skin Mr. Locust had peeled off my arms and legs in the car grew back slowly and tenderly. Erin was beside herself after waiting at the altar on her wedding day for Paolo to show, refusing to give up hope.

Like Paolo, the balance of my savings account disappeared. My bank said there was nothing they could do about it. The money was just gone, they said. Poof.

"Where did it go?" I said.

They said it was never there to begin with.

I told them about my deposits, said I had receipts. I demanded to speak with the manager.

The local branch manager's laugh was dry and peppery, familiar. "I was waiting for you to call," he said. "You don't think money just comes out of nowhere, do you?"

"I don't know," I admitted. "It seemed real."

"Think, for a second. You put money into a box, and more comes out. You didn't work for it, you did nothing. You were offered free money and you took it."

My phone dinged with a text from Penelope and I resisted the urge to hang up and check it.

"How I got the money isn't important," I said.

"Oh, it very much is. It's the whole point."

I tried to be angry, but I wasn't. My own avarice was at fault. "I wasn't deceiving anyone," I said, knowing I was pleading in vain.

"So?"

I'd read somewhere that trillions of neutrinos are passing through your body at any given moment, but you never feel them, or even notice. We needed to invent a new physics.

Penelope sent two more texts. I no longer wanted to call her back, because I knew, through her connection to me, something terrible had befallen her, or her children.

"What happens now?"

"That depends on what you do next. Consider this conversation your margin call."

"I'll pay it back," I said, pacing around my kitchen. I popped open the microwave door and closed it. I took Tyrone's half-empty bag of dry food from the cupboard. "Give me a month."

Mr. Locust sighed, a short hollow sound reminiscent of a distant lawnmower. "It doesn't work that way."

My body was shaking. I steadied myself on the counter, feeling my knees buckle. Something was wrong, I realized. Well, everything on the planet was wrong, but something locally was wrong, as well. Very wrong. Tyrone usually came sprinting on his stubby little legs from wherever he was when he heard the crinkle of the dog food bag.

Mr. Locust cleared his throat. "You still with me?"

I went into the bedroom and Tyrone's little body was on the bed.

"We've been on the phone 14 minutes now," Mr. Locust said, "and I charge by the quarter-hour. I'm happy to chat all day, but you may want to wrap this up."

I remembered someone once telling me how locusts were actually crickets, but a boost of some chemical, serotonin, in their brain *turned* them into a plague, changing their bodies and making them swarm. Like how Tyrone had metamorphosed suddenly from a happy dog into the stiff, malignant corpse on my bed, as if in a peaceful angle of repose, no longer disturbed by any heaving of his little lungs. It was only nature.

But the Money Box was not natural.

I felt a tickle in my left hand. A soft scratching. When I looked down I saw a chapstick-sized locust had buried its ovipositor under my skin. I watched in amazement as it laid eggs directly into the top of my hand, into the metacarpal bone.

It was suddenly excruciating, and I wanted to scream.

But I forced myself to stifle it. *Don't let him have the satisfaction*, I told myself.

I bit my lip, then my tongue. But I didn't make a sound.

Someone was profiting from the Money Box, but it wasn't me. My greed, and someone else's exploitation of it, was a fait accompli the minute I was born.

"It's not fair," I said finally, because I had nothing else to say.

"Don't be so sensitive," Mr. Locust said. "It's just business.

A market correction."

"But—"

"But nothing. You're the one who put yourself in this position."

"No I didn't."

But of course I had. The moment I heard about the Money Box I was bought in; I never even gave it a second thought. Someone else could read the fine print, I figured.

The phone read 14:51.

"The tide recedes," I said, petting Tyrone's body, "but comes back in stronger. Even the highest wall can't hold back the forces of history."

"Sure, tell yourself that. Vulgarities comfort the weak. But be honest with yourself, for once: all you do is take. You take, and you take, and you take. *You're* the plague. But go ahead and lie. Just remember that all debts must eventually be paid."

* * *

A month or so later my doorbell rang. To my shock it was Sanjeev, holding what looked like a birthday present. A bandage was wrapped around his head and face, like a blindfold, covering where his eyes must have been quite recently. There was still blood on the cloth. I didn't bother to ask what happened, because I already knew.

He handed me the gift without a word.

I wanted so desperately to see if he'd heard anything about Paolo, Erin, Steve, or Dee-Ann, but I found that I couldn't bring myself to utter their names.

And when I tried to offer him a tip, he refused, muttering "Pro bono, pro bono," like it was a prayer to ward off evil spirits.

After he left, I carried the present to my kitchen table,

dreading whatever was inside. And when I tore off the wrapping paper, there it was: a Money Box, hollow black, silent and odious, identical to Paolo's.

Maybe it was the same one, I don't know.

Resting on top of the Box was an ancient piece of parchment containing a square of faded purple script. My phone's translation app said it was Aramaic. The language of the lenders in the Temple. Despite my best intentions, my eyes were drawn to the words on my screen, which were now in English.

Welcome, new Steward. As of now, you are bound to this Trust. While in your possession, five new entities must use this Trust every lunation. Operation of this Trust without your oversight is forbidden. The Trust shall not be removed from your ownership except by an approved representative. The period of your stewardship of this Trust may last from two lunations to two lifetimes. You will know the approved representative when they come to retrieve the Trust, and the period of your stewardship is ended. Execute this Trust wisely, as failure to abide these rules will result in death.

* * *

This story first appeared in the After Dinner Conversation—June 2022 issue.

Discussion Questions

1. If you were invited to the party at the start of the story to use the Money Box, would you have gone, and would you have used it?

2. Do you agree with the story's theme against "unearned money?" How do you define "unearned money?"

3. Is making money from interest "unearned money?" What about making money from stock market investments, or more speculative financial instruments?

4. The story says, "power [like the Money Box] needs to be concentrated in few, competent hands; otherwise, society would devolve into an egalitarian, democratic wasteland." Do you agree or disagree with this statement?

5. What, if anything, should the narrator do now that he is the keeper of the Money Box? If you were in his place, would you lure others into the temptations of easy money to save yourself?

* * *

Lev's Pawn Shop

Megan Neary

* * *

In days gone by, it might have been said that Lev had had a vision, that he had been struck from his horse by the voice of God and seen the error of his ways. As it was, people said that he had gone a bit nutty in his old age, though it was unanimously agreed upon that it was the good sort of nutty he had gone. In actuality, Lev had simply realized he was going to die. Of course, he had always known that he would die someday, but someday had always been a long way off. Now, between the cough that stained all of his handkerchiefs red and the doctor's offer to help him find a nice hospice, someday had begun to sound an awful lot like tomorrow.

Lev, always a clever bookkeeper and a savvy businessman, began to examine his own account with God, and he found himself deep in the hole, having done quite a bit more bad than good. His sins were mostly related to his business, the business he had always been so proud to have built from the ground up, to have kept afloat and profitable through boom years and bust years alike. But now he found himself recalling Bible passages that spoke against usury, that implored charity, that said things like what you do to the least of these you do to me, and he remembered taking a wedding ring from a crying widow, remembered selling it the day she failed to buy it back, remembered the way she had begged for more time, remembered the way he had shrugged and said, "I'm sorry, ma'am. Business is business." He knew that shrug would see him cast down into Gehenna if he didn't do something to make up for it. And quick.

So, he decided to give everything back, and let the pawners keep the money he had given them for their little treasures. It was easy enough with the recent items. He got a few suspicious looks, a few nervous questions regarding how likely it was that he would change his mind, but mostly the people thanked him, hugged him, told him he had answered their prayers. He felt himself lessening his good deed debt, approaching the black, as it were.

But then he came to the older items: the necklaces and watches and guns and flowered China that had sat on his shelves for decades without being sold. He called a phone number that he found in his records written on yellowed paper in a dusty old crate, called it and asked to speak with Gloria, and was told that there was no Gloria there. He held the silver cross in his hand and almost cried. He wanted to give it back. Felt the chill of its chain to be an accusation of the chill in his heart. He remembered Gloria. He'd always had a good memory. Never forgot a face. Especially not this one. A beautiful young woman with red-rimmed blue eyes and holes in her shoes. Forty years ago. Forty years ago, she walked through his door and pulled the cross from beneath her dress, pulled it over her head, held it, for just a moment, gazed at it with the fond sadness of a mother saying goodbye to a grown child, then asked him what he could give her for it. And he drove a hard bargain. Gave her very little. He knew she would accept it. Had seen the desperation on her face. Had capitalized on that. For a while, she had come back every week to check on it. Then she had stopped. Her time was up. She had failed to pay him back. And he put it up for sale. Somehow, though, it never sold. Was picked up and admired often enough, but never made it through those doors. And now here he was, trying to return it, trying to find the pretty girl who, if she were still alive, would be an old woman by now. And how would he find her? She was not at her number. He resolved to try her address.

The next day, Lev stepped out of his shop and into the gently falling rain. There was a time when he would have turned around and gone back inside, fearful of developing a cold, but he felt now that walking through the rain to do a good deed would score him some bonus points. He'd be like that saint who stuck stones in his shoes. He walked through the rain, through the soggy newspapers and McDonald's bags that littered the sidewalk, past the rent-to-own shop and the payday loan center. When he reached the address, he found, in the place of the apartments that should have been there, an art gallery with a stack of garbage on display in the front window. A plaque beside it explained that the artist had spent seven years gathering trash from the alley behind his apartment in an attempt to create a sculpture of modern-day life. The sculpture included Coke cartons, used condoms, a single yellow glove, a string of purple beads, a CVS receipt so long it wrapped around the whole affair, and much, much more. Lev thought of the artist, picking through his neighbors' garbage, alone in a dark, rat-filled alley. Alone. And he thought perhaps it was the artist, rather than the garbage, who was a sculpture of modern-day life.

Lev walked back to the shop. Walked through the rain that had lost its luster, that had just begun to make his nose run and his feet cringe at the feel of squishy socks between his toes.

He hung the silver cross above his chair, hung it from a rusty nail dug into the once-white wall, sat beneath it, and imagined himself Damocles, except without the compensation of a kingdom.

He forced his mind to other thoughts, to the return of the other little treasures that still cluttered his shelves.

He took a now tuneless fiddle from its red-satin-lined box and held it to his chin. He held the bow above it, just out of touch, and, in his mind, he played beautifully. He had always wanted to be a musician. But his father—No. No time for that now. He was no musician. Never would be. But the man who had brought the fiddle in to his store all those years before, he was. He had played it. Had played it right there in front of the cash register. Had said he had to say goodbye, if it was all right. But he hadn't really been asking. Lev had stood and watched. Had been annoyed, at first, by the delay. But then the music. Oh, God, what a beautiful thing. And still Lev had taken the fiddle. Taken it and given the boy a pittance for it. He really was just a boy. Just a boy trying to be a man. Just a boy who had learned that he would be a father. Who had come looking for a ring. Who had brought his only possession of value with him. Who had been determined to do the right thing, no matter that it hurt like hell.

Lev called the number he found in his old record book. Called it and prayed while it rang. Begged for the chance to bring the fiddle home. When an old, grizzled voice answered, he asked to speak with Johnny Simpson. "No one's called me Johnny in years," answered the voice, "but that's me." Lev was surprised. It was stupid to be surprised. Of course the boy had aged. Just, somehow, he had expected a peach-fuzz-faced boy to be waiting, to be ready to take up the fiddle like no more than a day had passed. "I don't know if you remember me," Lev said, "but I have something of yours, and I'd like to give it back." "Who are you?" "This is Lev. From Lev's pawn shop." "Oh. I remember you," Johnny answered in a voice that belied no fond memories. "You talkin' 'bout my fiddle?" "Yes. I'd like to give it back. I could bring it to you. Any time." "Why would you want to do that? I never paid you back. It's yours. Fair and square." "Let's just say, I won't have any use for it where I'm headed. Could I please bring it to you?"

The next day, Lev drove out of the city and into the suburbs. He found a little blue house with a pretty red rose bush beside the immaculately white front door. He knocked. A woman with a pretty smile and lipstick as red as the roses answered. "You must be Mr. Lev," she said. "Please, come in." Lev followed her to a sitting room with flowered wallpaper and sat in the pink chair she offered him. Then, she disappeared. When she returned, she carried a plate of cookies. A man followed her with a pot of coffee and three mugs. It was Johnny. Johnny grown old. Johnny turned to John.

When the treats had been laid out on the table, John held out his hand. Lev stood up and shook it.

"So," said John, sitting down beside his wife on the couch

and taking her hand. "Thanks for coming way out here. I know it's a bit of a drive."

"I'm happy to do it. You have a beautiful home."

"Thank you," John said and he grinned so that he was Johnny again, for a moment. "I can tell you, it's a far cry from the one-room apartment above the Chinese takeout we started out in. You know, we moved into that place not a week after I went to your store. I got the ring. Hooked a priest. And that was that." He took his wife's hand gently from her lap and held it up toward Lev. "Guess you recognize the ring, huh? I've been trying to convince her to let me upgrade it, but my pleas have fallen on deaf ears."

"I could never part with it," the woman said, extracting her hand from John's and admiring the little speck of diamond set in carefully polished silver. "It reminds me of where we started. Of the joy that can come from struggle, so long as you struggle beside someone you love."

John bent over and gave her a peck on the cheek, then quickly pulled away.

"I'm glad to see things worked out between you," Lev said. "It makes me feel a little less rotten."

"Why should you feel rotten? It's not as if you stole the fiddle."

"Isn't it though? At least a little? I just can't stop remembering the way you played it. Played it right there in the store while I tapped my fingers and sighed, pretended impatience. I wanted you to play forever."

"That's very kind of you to say, but I was never anything special. Not really. It was just a hobby."

"Do you have a new fiddle now?"

"No. I'm afraid I gave music up. Life gets busy, you know. Work. Kids. Everything."

"I'm sorry to hear that," Lev said and he was. So sorry he might have cried. So sorry he might have lost his coffee across the pink couch. "Well," he went on, standing up, "it's been a real pleasure to meet you. And I thank you for your hospitality." He handed the violin case to John and shook his hand once more.

Outside the front door, standing beside the thorn-ridden rose bush, Lev heard a sweet, clear strain come from the violin. Just one note. Just the first in a long line of tune ups. And it was so beautiful.

Lev's grandson came by the shop the next day. He'd been sent by his mother—who had come by the shop a few days before and seen Lev balanced precariously on a ladder, attempting to clear off his top shelves—to help the old man. He wasn't thrilled to be spending his Saturday in a dusty old shop with a dusty old man, but, once Lev explained his desire to track down the items' original owners, he woke up, sat up straight, pulled out his phone and began to google the people Lev couldn't find. He tried the owner of the silver cross first, but found no leads. Lev felt the nail that held it sigh with its weight. But he did have luck finding the owner of an emerald brooch. Lev remembered her, too. She'd walked into the shop just before closing, hair a greasy mess, eyes sunk deep, surrounded by thick black shadows, face so thin he could see every bone, shaking, shivering despite the summer heat, fidgeting with a thread on her dirty gray sleeve, setting the brooch down and asking in a voice that sounded like it was far out of practice, "What'll you give me for this?" She never came back. Not even to check on it the first week, make sure it was still there, like people so often did. And now here she was, smiling at him through a Facebook profile, barely recognizable, her eyes clear and happy, her face filled out, her hair clean and shining. Lev dictated to his grandson who messaged her and explained the situation. She responded immediately, excitedly, using a lot of emojis that Lev's grandson showed him and tried to explain. They arranged to meet the next day at a coffee shop down the street.

When Lev got there, he saw her, sitting at a table beside the windows, fidgeting with the brown paper hand protector that encircled her cup. Another sat across from it in front of the empty seat.

"I hope black's okay," she said when she saw Lev, then she smiled and gave a little laugh. "You are Lev, aren't you? I'm Mary."

"Nice to meet you, Mary," Lev said, and they shook hands. "And black coffee is perfect. Thank you."

"No, thank you. I can't tell you what this means to me. I've been searching for that brooch for years. I knew I sold it, but I didn't know where. You wouldn't believe how many pawn shops there are in this city, just in this neighborhood for god's sake. And then I gave up. Assumed someone had bought it. Couldn't keep killing myself over it. And then your message. And her birthday was just last week. It's almost. It's almost a sign. Oh, I'm sorry," and she looked down, resumed her fidgeting, "I'm talking too much."

"Not at all," said Lev, "but whose birthday is it? Were you hoping to give her the brooch for a gift? It really is beautiful."

"Not exactly. It was my grandmother's birthday last week. When I got sober, I always planned to find it and give it back to her. But I was too late. She's gone. But I. Well, I don't know. I think she'd still like to know I got it back for her. Brought it back to the family. Her own mother gave it to her the night before her wedding. She didn't have an easy life, but she always managed to hold on to it. And then I stole it. Stole it from her. From the only person in the world who would have anything to do with me when I was like that." She began to cry. "I'm sorry," she said, wiping at her eyes and nose roughly, "I've told this story in enough meetings, but it never gets easier."

"You have nothing to apologize for, honey. It's okay. You can let it out."

And then, somehow, they were standing. Standing there beside their cold coffees, standing among the crowded tables. Lev was holding her, and he was rocking back and forth, back and forth, and patting her back, moving his hand in circles, remembering how he used to rock his babies, how he never did it enough, how he only did it until he could hand them off to their mother, and he was glad to do this now, to rock this woman and not to want to hand her off at all.

When they sat back down, he gave her the brooch and they drank their cold coffees and talked about little things and could almost not believe that they had held each other.

Lev went back to the shop and sat in his chair. He thought of the people he had met, of the many others he had failed to find. He felt the cross hanging above him, hanging by a thread. He knew now he would not find the woman, knew he would find no one else. Knew that he had failed, that he had done more bad than good, that he was still deep in debt. Thought maybe he could be forgiven just the same, loved just the same. He fell asleep and did not wake.

* * *

This story first appeared in the After Dinner Conversation—December 2022 issue.

Discussion Questions

1. Stories frequently consist of someone doing a wrong, then working hard to correct it in the end. Who deserves more credit, those that attempt to correct their wrongs, or those who quietly never commit the wrongs in the first place?

2. Lev's desire to correct his past wrongs is directly related to his pending death and his desire to "examine his own account with God." Given his motivation, do you think Lev should get credit for his recent good deeds?

3. For each sale, Lev provided valuable access to money when the person was in desperate need. Do you think Lev did anything wrong as a pawn broker? Do business people have a duty to sometimes pay more than the going rate?

4. Of the returned items, which do you find the most heartbreaking and why?

5. Is it ever too late to do good? Is the good diminished by the length of time you wait and others suffer?

* * *

Bugs In the Valley

Saba Waheed

* * *

"So, did you fix nature?" I leaned over the stool at the bar. "Excuse me?"

"Ethics class," I said. Amaya stared at me blankly. "Stanford," I continued, "you argued science for the greater good means editing genes to improve humanity, population control to preserve resources. Nature botched the job..."

"And we should fix it," Amaya said, her expression still stoic. "Right, you called me a eugenicist."

I smiled but she merely turned back to her drink. She had the same loner energy I remembered from college. I never saw her at parties, or academic clubs, never saw her date anyone. I'd see her walking alone, her head leaning slightly forward as if her mind was already at the destination. Amaya was the kind of beautiful that didn't know she was, or didn't care.

"You were right." I motioned to the bartender for another drink. "If we have the resources to design a better world, then we should do it."

"I'm always right," she said without turning to me. I took my drink and went back to the table with my work team. I watched as Amaya remained at the bar alone the rest of the night. She didn't use her phone, she didn't read anything, she never even glanced back to see who else was in the bar. She just looked forward, finishing one drink after another.

When I said goodbye to the last of my friends, I went back to the bar.

"You work in the Valley?"

"Yes."

"Yeah, me too." I waited for her to say more, but nothing. "Tech? Business?"

"Medical."

"What company?"

"Can't say."

"I work in tech. Not R&D, but the business side. My team and I were celebrating tonight. We got driverless cars approved statewide."

For the first time, she turned and looked at me. "I thought that program was dead."

"It was." I sat down on the stool and told her my strategies—reshape the conversation, get buy-in from politicians, override regulation, create some new laws, repeat.

"One day my work will be ready for the world," she said. When she looked at me, it felt like she was taking all of me with her. Then she turned away and the feeling was gone. She signaled to the bartender and asked for her check. It was abrupt. "Good chatting." She put down the cash and walked away.

Later that week I used my connections to figure out where she worked. When I discovered it was Gamelin, one of the most heavily invested medical labs in the Valley, I knew she was working on something big. A few weeks later, Amaya reached out to me.

I arrived at a local cafe and found her already seated. "I hear you're the best and can get anything to the market." I was pleased my reputation had caught her attention. "Join my team."

"You haven't told me what you do."

"You have to say yes first."

My success in the Valley was knowing when to jump.

I went through a series of background checks, non-disclosure agreements, and interviews. Once approved, Amaya asked me to attend a briefing for the company's board and top investors. Her assistant loaded up the presentation and Amaya steadily went through their work. They built medical nanotech, an application she referred to simply as 'the bugs', that could safely enter the body.

"Have you ever seen those tanks with fish that eat away the dead skin on your feet?" Her gaze landed on me and I smiled. "They have the ability to go after dead cells while leaving the healthy ones behind. Our bugs do the same. They roam through the body until they find a malignant tumor and then eat away at it until it's gone."

When the presentation was over, the room lit up. "We cured cancer! We did it."

"Wait, wait, there's one more thing." The board quieted and turned back to Amaya. "The bugs cannot be permitted to stay in the body. They themselves continue to replicate to a point where they can take over and become a sort of plague. So, we program them to die after a few replications and the body disposes of them. In all of our cases to date, the cancer returns."

"It's temporary?" asked one of the board members.

"Yes, but it works for years, anywhere from five to ten years. That's a lot of time with family, and far better quality of life, not stuck in chemo or radiation."

"Why not inject them again?" asked another board member.

"There's a limited supply and until we can figure that part out, our strategy is to spread it out, broaden the benefits." This is when she looked right at me. "Let's give more people a few more good years, rather than give only a few people many more years."

I met Amaya later to develop the plan. She told me how she'd started to build the technology when she was in graduate school. It had worked in animals and that success got her a position and a ridiculous amount of money and resources at the Gamelin Lab. But, for years, no matter what she did, the human body rejected the bugs.

"The technology alone wasn't enough, so I started doing all kinds of animal and plant experiments." She'd brought in geologists, environmentalists, herbalists, zoologists, and botanists and told them to bring in anything that could mimic cells.

"Nature."

"Yes," she smiled. "We needed nature. I met a plant specialist who brought me rare plants from around the world. One plant, ironically called the 'corpse flower,' worked. It gave the bugs an organic cover and the human body didn't see them as invaders. But the plant only exists in one part of the world, and we haven't figured out how to grow it here in the lab. But we will."

Amaya's project gave me new focus. My team created the distribution strategy. A project like this would take years to reach the public but I leveraged every single one of my contacts to fast track the process. Amaya would meet with me regularly to discuss the approach. She wanted it to reach patients with the least access to treatment. It was during one of these meetings that she told me how both her parents died.

"Freshman year of college. Cancer. One right after the other." She was sitting in an office chair across from me. It was a moment of vulnerability I hadn't seen in her. "Thanks, nature."

"That's why you were so..."

"I was so what?" She looked up, a wall back up.

"Nothing."

I shocked the entire Valley when I lined up all the necessary approvals in three months. We held a press conference and had media from every part of the country, every part of the world. None of my tech projects had received this kind of exposure. Amaya and I celebrated over drinks that night. She was glowing. She looked at me with such fullness and light. "You did it," she said.

"We did it," I replied. We were at a bar, sitting on stools side by side. "Our world is better off with all the new technologies. Streets are safer, we have more access to food, and now this—bugs that can fight nature's greatest threat to our bodies."

"I just need to make it bigger. I'm close. I can feel it." Then she turned to me and said abruptly, "Come home with me."

And I did.

A few weeks later we found out she was pregnant. I thought back to that night and the details were fuzzy. Were we careful, was I too drunk to care, had she encouraged me to go forward anyway? "I want to do this," she said, when we met to discuss what to do. "I won't make the time otherwise. I have no expectations of you. We can make it contractual, so you're in the clear."

"I want to do it." I said it before I had fully processed what that meant.

I was in the hospital room when Jayde was born. I laid her on my chest and I couldn't feel the difference in our bodies. I looked at this little being that was part me and part Amaya and the world felt whole. Amaya took time off from work and it was probably the only extended period she had ever spent away from her project. I would come over in the evenings, relieving her so she could rest. By the time Jayde was five, I had moved in and we were functioning as a family.

As Jayde grew, so did her curiosity. One day we were out sitting in a neighborhood park. It was a warm Saturday afternoon. Amaya was in the lab and I had taken the day off. "What does Mama do?"

"Your mama, she's the brains behind the bugs."

"Ew." Jayde scowled.

"No, these are super bugs that kill the bad guy cells."

"And what do you do?"

"I create the path for the bugs to go from the lab into our bodies." Jayde looked at me questioningly. "You see that coffeebot that knew exactly what I wanted to drink before I even walked up? People were afraid of robots and didn't want them making our drinks or cleaning our homes. I changed that, changed the way people think about machines and what they are willing to accept. Now, look, they are everywhere."

As the years passed, our inboxes were filled with messages from individuals and family members. Amaya would bring a few home and we would sit down with Jayde in the evenings and read them together. But I could feel Amaya's frustration in not being able to get those families more time, and not being able to get the bugs to more families.

She wasn't the only one feeling impatient.

In the tenth year of the program, one of the project investors came to my office. "The whole thing is a money pit." I knew this already. The hospital program didn't generate revenue and the production and research was costly. "We can give it a year, after that, the research ends, and we put the bugs on the market."

I told Amaya about the meeting. "If it goes on the market, only some people will have access to it—people like my parents would be left out." There was desperation in her voice. "I can't make the science go any faster."

I couldn't handle seeing Amaya so upset. I reached out to the investor to negotiate more time. When I got to his office, he was sitting with another man wearing a lab coat—Amaya's number two.

"We will fund the project if you change the business plan." He pushed forward a new non-disclosure agreement. If I shared anything about our deal, the entire project would be defunded— the research, the production, the patients. If I didn't sign it, the entire project would be defunded in a year anyway. "You can't tell Amaya," he repeated as I signed.

He directed me to the lab. A technician took me into a plain room with a table and two chairs. She pulled up my sleeve, swabbed it with alcohol and, with an unusually large syringe, injected me. "That's it?" I asked. It was less than a prick. Over the next few weeks, I started to feel slight changes. I could run a little faster, my mind felt clearer, and I could feel a whirlpool of energy throughout my body.

I went back to the investor's office.

"You get it now, right?"

"I get that something is happening."

Amaya's number two explained it. "A few years into the project, we noticed that people who had the bug, it wasn't just that the cancer was gone, they were getting healthier than they were before. There was a youthfulness that came back, and parts of the body that had been aging, reversed. It turns out, the bugs weren't stopping at the cancer, they were zipping through the system repairing everything—from organs to decomposing cells."

"Meaning?"

"There's never a moment of cellular senescence. The bugs keep you healthy and they keep you young."

"Amaya's known for some years about this 'side effect'," the investor said.

"Why are you telling me this?"

"You're the best strategist we have," he said, leaning back in his chair. "And, you'll do anything to make sure the project survives."

He was right. I rounded up a dozen billionaires from the Valley and beyond. When they heard what the bug could do, one of them turned to the Gamelin Lab investor and asked, "You built an anti-aging bug?" The investor nodded, a huge grin on his face.

He stood up, as if giving a toast. "Friends, here we are, on the cusp of change. To everlasting life!" The room crowed in delight.

I was miserable holding this back from Amaya but a few days later, she came home and told me that her budget had increased. "Whatever you did, thank you," she said.

As the months turned into a year and a year into many, my body had changed, or rather, it stopped changing. Don't get me wrong, a bus could still run me over, and the bugs would do nothing for that. But my body was healthy and without the specter of aging and disease, I felt bigger, stronger, and became less risk-averse. With a few more billionaires, I garnered even more resources. I eyed other companies, finding the top developers and scientists at the forefront of new ideas and technology, and bought them.

Amaya and I became distant. She went into a dark hole every time she failed to replicate the corpse flower. Meanwhile, I was on the rise, and was bringing more and more technologies into the public. I was the most sought-after person in the Valley.

When Jayde was ready for college, she chose an art school in New York. I was disappointed. I thought she would follow one of our careers. Amaya and I took a few days off to settle her into her dorm. We explored the city and ate meals at different restaurants. It should have been a joyful family trip, but Amaya snapped at me and grew more irritable as the weekend went by.

She was quiet on the way back, staring out the plane window even though it was dark. When we got home, I made myself a drink. Amaya watched me from the kitchen counter. The silence between us was enormous.

She finally spoke. "Who told you?"

"Told me what?" I said as I took a full swig of the whiskey, clearing half the glass. "Why didn't you tell me?"

"I didn't tell anyone."

"I am not anyone. You should've trusted me."

"I was right not to."

"You weren't complaining when your budget increased." I looked at her sideways and I could tell she was brimming with anger.

"And what was the purpose of you taking it?"

I was surprised that she knew. "I needed to understand how it worked," I mumbled.

She went into her bag and pulled out a reader. She pushed aside my drink and placed it in front of me. It was a message from a mother whose daughter Nori was diagnosed with stage four brain cancer. Even with all the science today, she had only weeks. "That dose in you could've given that mother another decade with her daughter."

I scrolled down and noticed her place on the waitlist. "She's next in line for the bugs."

"She's dead." Amaya stepped back. "No more doses for you or the others."

"Then your project is dead," I said. Her face contorted and I saw that she knew I was right. She walked out of the kitchen and I heard the bedroom door slam.

I slept in the guest bedroom. I believed once we got some rest, we could talk about it again. When I woke up and walked into the kitchen, she was already drinking coffee. "I want you to move out."

"Look, I know I shouldn't have taken it."

"Out," she said without any emotions.

"It was only once."

Amaya didn't respond. She got up, grabbed her bag and left for work. I went to a hotel and figured we'd talk about it after a few days. But she refused to return my messages and they wouldn't let me into the lab to see her.

The doses the investors received were ending. I could feel the bugs leaving my system. My body felt heavy, weighed down by gravity. I felt lethargic and my mind was cluttering up. Worst of all, my emotions were palpable. I needed to talk to Amaya and we had to figure this out. If we didn't renew the doses, I didn't see how we could continue the project. Now that she knew, I wanted to work together with her to find a solution. I waited outside of our house. When she saw me, her face glowed with anger.

"We have to talk," I said.

"People died because of you."

"And many more are going to live because of me."

"You have an overblown understanding of your importance."

"Look, just listen to me, we have to figure out what to do next."

"There is no 'we' in this project. The bugs are mine."

"They aren't yours."

"You. You are...just some middle man."

Now I was angry. "What did you see in me anyway?"

"You...you just happened." She pushed past me and went into the unit. I hated her at that moment. Something was finally stripped away and I was seeing Amaya for who she was—she didn't care for anything but the bugs.

The next day, I went back to the lab and got a new dose. As soon as they pushed the syringe, I felt big again. I knew it wasn't possible, the bugs didn't move that fast, but even the idea that they were there, fortifying my body, gave me strength.

And with the bugs inside of me, Amaya mattered less.

I renewed another round of the bugs to the billionaires to keep Amaya's project funded. I still believed in its mission even if she didn't believe in me. But I brought in additional donors to support my expansion into other sectors. I was taking over more companies, buying up all the patents so that all new tech had to go through me. I placed some friendly faces in city councils, state and federal governments. The tech world was thriving and I was leading the charge.

I shouldn't have been surprised when the media leak happened. I suspected Amaya. Journalists reported that the bug program had shifted from hospitals to wealthy clients. Protesters staged demonstrations outside of our offices and labs, demanding justice. "Bugs for the sick, not for the rich." I worked with our security to take care of it. We could access their plans through any one of their home or handheld devices and countered or preempted their actions. When a few of the protest leaders received a dose of bugs, they quickly backed off. We initiated a public lottery program—to bring in a few non-elites. You didn't have to have cancer, or be rich, to get the bugs.

I could imagine Amaya's rage, but I wasn't around to witness it.

The next time I saw her was in the boardroom. She had sprinkles of white hair that shined under the light. A part of me hoped she'd take the bugs, even if just to fight me for a few more years. When it was time to present her findings to the board, she stood at the edge of the conference table, looked around the room and then said that there were no new updates. They had failed again to replicate the corpse flower.

Amaya kept her eyes moving, scanning each of the faces. When she got to mine, she stopped. She stared at me, and I saw recognition in her eyes. She knew that I knew that she was lying. She dared me to say something. I dropped my gaze and she moved on.

Afterwards, I saw her in the hallway. "Why didn't you tell them about the breakthrough?"

"They don't deserve the bugs."

As she turned to walk away, I grabbed her arm. "You will lose this project if you don't tell them."

"I will lose this project if I tell them."

A few weeks later, I was walking by the bar, the one where we first ran into each other decades ago now. Amaya was sitting alone, her drink mostly full. Maybe she felt me because she turned around and our eyes met. I saw something in her face, something familiar. Buried under all that rage, what we had, it was there. It was still there. I moved to open the door but she turned away, back to her drink.

I came home to my empty unit. There were women I could call but I didn't feel like it. I put my bag and jacket down and powered down all the bots and gadgets. The wind was pounding against the windows, the night rageful. I grabbed a beer and some cheese out of the fridge, and pulled out a box of crackers. At the kitchen counter, I ate quietly. Maybe I was nearing the end of a dose. Maybe a disease had found its way into my body and the bugs were working harder. Or maybe, it was seeing Amaya.

I was the most powerful man in the Valley, but I felt like I had just landed at the bottom of a pit. I got into bed and couldn't sleep. My mind was racing, searching for a way to turn this around. With sufficient supply, we wouldn't have to choose anymore. I needed Amaya to listen to me. I felt my eyes grow heavy just as the sun was coming up. As I was about to finally fall asleep, I was bombarded by a series of alerts in my ear implant.

Amaya had died in a lab explosion.

The FBI was at the site by the time I arrived. They told me that Amaya and a lab technician were working early that morning. There was some kind of accident and both of them died. Only part of the lab was harmed but it was the side that held the components needed to replicate the flower. Amaya had cordoned off staff access to the research long ago so that no one knew the whole process. They would have to start over.

The next day, an FBI agent was sitting at my desk flipping through a series of photos, messages and documents. The agent said that they had evidence that Amaya was planning to blow up the lab but the technician caught her. He was able to subvert the operation. He sacrificed his life to save the lab. She was attempting to destroy the research and entire production infrastructure for the bugs.

"That's not possible, she lived for the program," I said.

"Our understanding, sir, is that the company was going to take the program away from her after she replicated the flower. They had already alerted us to the possibility of her doing something like this."

It was no accident.

Amaya's name was now associated with terrorists.

Not the founder of the bugs.

I went to visit Jayde. She didn't believe any of the news reports, and I didn't have the heart to tell her about the evidence.

We held a private memorial and spent a few mournful days together. I took the cross-country bullet train home. I sat in the cocktail lounge. It was set up retro style with ornate sofas and tables. Classical music played softly in the background. I found a seat in a booth by a window. The BarBot came by and I ordered a whiskey on the rocks. I took a sip and turned my head to the side to look outside. We were going so fast that the landscape was a blur and yet the ride was smooth. The bullet train was one of my company's initiatives. I had moved so many stalled projects, brought technology to a new apex. The bugs made it possible. I made it happen. Here I was running circles around Amaya's righteousness but she never saw what I was doing. I looked around the cabin. No one was complaining.

I went back for a new dose of the bug. We revised our distribution system. There were tiers, 1-dose, 3-doses, 5-doses and so on which we would use strategically. We distributed to businessmen, to heads of states—I believed it brought peace and kept commerce strong. Nothing stopped war like bugs.

Jayde and I became closer after Amaya's death. We met regularly and it was during one of her art exhibits that I realized that she was becoming older than me. I offered her the bugs.

"I don't know. Do I want to extend my life?"

"It's not about living longer, it's the clarity and succinctness of that living. You won't be muddled by fear. You will stay you, but a more effective you."

Jayde gave me a considering look. "But Mom never took it."

"It was a different time then."

"How many artists have it?"

"You'd be the first."

The next wave of public backlash was bigger. People complained that we were using the bugs to manipulate politics, fast track our own projects, and distribute resources unevenly, leaving people at the bottom suffering. The newest round of resistance was harder to quell. They were leaderless and we couldn't quite figure out who to detain or retain with bugs. Instead, we did a broad scramble of public communications and built a counter media campaign—the public understood that centralizing the bugs is what brought them the conveniences and technological advances.

What I didn't expect was Jayde's sympathy for them. She visited me via hologram at my office one afternoon. "You're misusing the bugs." She stood there like Amaya's ghost.

"Jayde, don't make accusations," I said dismissively.

"You called the military on protesters."

"What, who told you that?" We'd had a hard media blackout on that approach.

"Is it true?" When I didn't respond, she phased out.

Jayde continued to fight with me and started to cancel on our monthly dinners. When we would meet, she'd insist that the bug program was corrupt.

"You're being manipulated," I told her.

"I have the mental clarity that came with the bugs," she retorted. It was true and that is what surprised me. With the bugs, I thought she would understand them and their power. Instead, she was becoming the spokesperson for their end.

She joined Back to the Basics, a radical group of luddites that wanted to slow down tech and science and end the bugs program. She removed all tech gadgets from her life making it impossible for me to track her. I thought she would come back when she needed a new dose, and that by then the rebelliousness would end.

The years moved slower after Jayde cut off communication with me. Even with the bugs, I felt a kind of heaviness. I thought of having another child, and had been in relationships where that was possible, but it was never about kids, it was about Jayde. It was harder to stay engaged. The world consisted of just a few companies that were being run by those of us on the bugs.

I felt my first bit of joy in a decade when Jayde reached out. I met her on a farm plot in the South. She laid in a bare and simple room. Each strand of white hair, each wrinkle signaled her departure. I begged her to take the bugs, "We can have a few more years together."

"No," she said simply. "You get off them."

Just like her mother, stubborn to the end.

I held a private cremation, but a few of her friends showed up. I knew they were from the rebellion. I was going to ask them to leave, but they filed in quietly, holding their own grief. We stood together, saying our goodbyes.

Afterwards, I walked to a nearby park. There was a brisk wind, greenery, sounds of birds, but it was all holograms and metal. So many parts of nature were dying or gone. For the first time in a long time, I thought of Amaya. And I knew, deep in my core, this wasn't what she envisioned when she said we should fix nature.

A young man from Jayde's group approached me. He sat next to me on the park bench. His features were dark, his eyes had a familiarity to them. Like Amaya's. Or maybe I was imagining it.

"She was working with the movement," he said.

"I know."

"Not Jayde. Amaya." I looked at him but didn't say anything. "When she figured out how to replicate the flower, she was going to give it to us. She wanted to put it in the hands of the people." He waited for a response but I stared out into the park. "It was always meant to be for healing and easing pain. You turned it into something else."

"You know nothing, you're a child."

He scoffed. "We have been passing down stories through each generation. We never died. Just like you." He stood up, ready to leave. "Your company killed her; they knew she had figured out how to replicate the flower."

"That's not true." It couldn't be true. It was a trick to confuse me, to exploit my grief. I knew because this is what I did to them.

"They never wanted it to be mass-produced, so they got rid of her."

"They needed her."

"Only until they understood her research, after that, she was disposable. Just like the bugs in your body." He walked away and joined his group.

My hands were clenched tight and I couldn't move. I looked around and the park had emptied out. I walked back to the crematorium and got the urn with Jayde in it. When I got to my car, it started up on its own. The car door opened, slapping my hand, and the urn dropped. The ashes fell to the ground, flying everywhere. I got on my knees and gathered what I could but bits had fallen through a grate leading to the underground roadways. I put my head down and for the first time that I could remember, I cried.

The bugs had given me life, and the bugs had taken life away from me.

I stood up and leaned against the car, barely able to catch my breath. I didn't want a life that didn't have Jayde in the world. I needed to join her, even if it meant meeting her in emptiness. And I hoped that maybe Amaya would be there too.

"I'm coming," I said.

* * *

This story first appeared in the After Dinner Conversation—October 2021 issue.

Discussion Questions

1. Do you agree with the statement "...science for the greater good means editing genes to improve humanity" or should science not attempt to improve humanity through gene editing?

2. Assuming the "bugs" could never be produced at scale, how should they be distributed to the public? Should they go to the highest bidder, go to the most needy, or be distributed in some other way? Should the age of the person be a factor, that is to say, should a very old person with a terminal disease be given the "bugs?"

3. Isn't it reasonable that medical investors would want to maximize the profits from their research investments? Is it wrong that individual investors fund research the government is unable, or unwilling, to invest in?

4. What do you think would happen, how do you think it would be handled, if a company actually invented a medicine that could stop the aging process? How should it work in a just society? Why can't it work that way?

5. Is it appropriate for companies and/or governments to use (*or withhold*) access to medicine to encourage good behavior and improve global stability?

* * *

Author Information

The Pool

Celia Lisset Alvarez is a writer and educator from Miami, Florida. She holds an MFA in creative writing from the University of Miami and has four collections of poetry: *Shapeshifting*, *The Stones*, *Multiverses*, and *Bodies & Words*. Her most recent publication is the anthology *SMEOP 2: HOT* and has forthcoming work in *Talon Review*. She was the editor of the *Prospectus: A Literary Offering*. *www.celialissetalvarez.com*

First Gold

Bob Beach's stories have appeared in more than a dozen publications, including *The Saturday Evening Post*, *The Woven Tale Press*, and *The Penmen Review*. He spent many years as a writer and designer for print and film in advertising and enjoyed a brief career as a fine artist. He also taught for many years at Bowling Green State University. He holds BSc and MFA degrees from BGSU and is currently enrolled in the MA Creative Writing program at Wilkes University. He resides in Toledo, Ohio.

Pandora's Dreams

Peter Beaumont lives in Melbourne, Australia and is an environmental consultant and writer. Peter studied philosophy at university and is constantly fascinated by the practical and theoretical questions involved in the endless moral and ethical dilemmas that humans face.

Cicada

Ishan Dylan is a conservation biologist and fiction writer from the Chesapeake area. His work is forthcoming in *Exposition Review's* 'Lines' issue. X (Twitter) *@IshanDylan*; *www.ishandylan.com*

Claim

Dr. Fiona Ennis lectures in Literature and Philosophy in Waterford Institute of Technology, Ireland. She has won the Molly Keane Creative Writing Award and her work has been published in *Sonder*, *The Honest Ulsterman* and a number of anthologies. Her fiction has also been shortlisted for the Bristol Short Story Prize and highly commended in the Manchester Fiction Prize and the Seán O Faoláin International Short Story Award. X (Twitter) *@FionaEnnis3*

Thorn

Erik Fatemi lives in Arlington, Virginia. A former newspaper editor and columnist, he now lobbies the federal government on behalf of nonprofit health groups. His fiction has also been published in *JMWW*, *Identity Theory*, and *WWPH Writes*. X (Twitter) *@ErikFatemi.*

Guilt-Edge Security

James A. Hartley is an Australian author now based in Germany by way of the UK. Although an occasional poet, his primary focus has always been short fiction. He feels that it is there that the author is naked on the page and that in the short story, there really is nowhere to hide. His works have appeared in Australia, Canada, and the USA and been translated into both Greek and Italian.

The Money Box

Phillip Scott Mandel is the founder and managing editor of *Abandon Journal*. His work has appeared in *The Gettysburg Review, Passages North, Hobart, Bull*, and many other places. He has an MFA from Texas State University and lives in Austin, Texas.

Lev's Pawn Shop

Megan Neary is a teacher and writer in Columbus, Ohio. Her work has appeared in various journals and literary magazines, including: *The Amethyst Review*, *The Cleveland Review of Books*, and *The Schuylkill Valley Journal*. She co-edits *Flyover Country Literary Magazine*. X (Twitter) *@meganneary2*

Bugs In the Valley

Saba Waheed's work has appeared in *Water-Stone Review* (Fiction Prize winner), *The Southeast Review* (Pushcart-nominated), *Bellingham Review, Lunch Ticket, Cosmonauts Avenue, Big Echo*, and others. She was a Caldera 2020 Artist-in-Residence. She co-produces the podcast *Re:Work*, winner of a Gracie by the Alliance for Women in Media. Saba works as the research director at the UCLA Labor Center using research as a tool to elevate community stories. X (Twitter) *@sabawaa*

Additional Information

Reviews

If you enjoyed reading these stories, please consider doing an online review. It's only a few seconds of your time, but it is very important in continuing the series. Good reviews mean higher rankings. Higher rankings mean more sales and a greater ability to release stories.

Print Books

https://www.afterdinnerconversation.com

Purchase our growing collection of print anthologies, "Best of," and themed print book collections. Available from our website, online bookstores, and by order from your local bookstore.

Podcast Discussions/Audiobooks

https://www.afterdinnerconversation.com/podcastlinks

Listen to our podcast discussions and audiobooks of After Dinner Conversation short stories on Apple, Spotify, or wherever podcasts are played. Or, if you prefer, watch the podcasts on our YouTube channel or download the .mp3 file directly from our website.

Patreon

https://www.patreon.com/afterdinnerconversation

Get early access to short stories and ad-free podcasts. New supporters also get a free digital copy of the anthology *After Dinner Conversation– Season One*. Support us on Patreon!

Book Clubs/Classrooms

https://www.afterdinnerconversation.com/book-club-downloads

After Dinner Conversation supports book clubs! Receive free short stories for your book club to read and discuss!

Social

Connect with us on Facebook, YouTube, Instagram, TikTok, Substack, and Twitter.